Nostrana

Flavours from
my Italian
kitchen garden

Nostrana

BRI DIMATTINA

Photography by Lottie Hedley

HarperCollins*Publishers*

Contents

This book is in the order by which things appear in my own garden, but everybody's garden is different. My year starts with the kōwhai tree on the edge of my courtyard blossoming and filling with raucous tūī. It's my signal that the soil is warm enough to start planting out my tomatoes, beans and other 'after the last frost' items. I really recommend finding these clues in your own garden to guide you, and keeping a diary.

Introduction

Nostrana is Italian for 'homegrown', and that pretty much sums up this book.

Gardening crept up on me. I never really referred to myself as a gardener – I'm not sure why, my kitchen windowsill has always been littered with cuttings and seedlings and small caches of seedheads. Even when I was flat broke and renting, there was a kitchen garden with a few things in it. But it was just something I did, like any other run-of-the-mill thing around the house. There is no single moment I became a gardener; I've always been this way. Maybe I inherited it.

My poppa grew tomatoes in Nelson in the 1940s for the household kitchen, but also as a job. So the smell of a brushed-against tomato plant is bit nostalgic for me. I often snatch ripe ones off the vine and demolish them right in front of the plant.

Poppa came to New Zealand as a 12-year-old, travelling on his own from Stromboli, a tiny island north of Sicily in the middle of the Tyrrhenian Sea. The island is a live volcano, constantly smoking, and often draws cruise ships to witness the lava bursts leaping against the night sky. It wasn't uncommon for the hillside to catch fire and, during an especially fierce set of eruptions, everyone would get in the row boats perched on the shore and row out to sea to wait it out. The village is at the base of the volcano. There is black sand on the shore and not much in the way of flora and fauna, due to the regular fires caused by stray lava rocks spat out by the volcano. The houses are built from these rocks, plastered over to create a quaint whitewashed village with grape vines and bougainvillea growing over the courtyards and gates. The only building of any great substance is the cathedral and its courtyard in the middle of the village. On my first visit, my surname, DiMattina (uncommon by New Zealand standards), was suddenly everywhere. I visited the cemetery thinking I could trace some ancestry, but my surname was on too many headstones to even start.

My nonna was from Naples. Her family emigrated in the early 1900s to Wellington, then she and my poppa moved to Nelson when my father was born. Church on Sundays would be followed by large, lingering lunches – the main meal of the day. We made visits to friends and neighbours, all recent arrivals to New Zealand who were finding their feet, often refugees with similar backgrounds and homeland memories. Nonna was part of a community in Nelson called 'The Wood', who helped ensure new arrivals were welcomed, finding them a place to live, filling their pantries and finding work. Many lifelong friendships were made through this and some have lasted for generations.

ABOVE *Me, 18 months old in Poppa's garden with a peg bag full of beans.*

6

Everyone shared the things they grew, and swapped recipes. Nonna's book is full of handwritten recipes and collected notes tucked into the back cover. Some are labelled 'Moll', 'Dorothy' or 'Eileen' – it's very poignant reading these. It sends me straight back there in my memories of the house and garden, to the exact spot where I first tasted something.

Life was substantially better in New Zealand, compared to where they had come from, at least up until the Second World War. At that time Italians, even naturalised citizens, were considered enemy aliens and generally despised and accused of spying, so were sent to Somes Island. Italian families rallied together in their small communities to support each other, most of them without a main breadwinner, so it was tough to get by for a few years. The self-sustainability of a small immigrant community became a form of food security – even if it wasn't said out loud. There was never any hint of disgruntlement about this phase of history spoken in front of me, but you picked it up at school and in the slightly derogatory Italian nicknames you encountered (or being told by HR managers how to spell your own surname), so I can only imagine what it was like for them.

Nonna and Poppa had an enviable food garden – apart from a small flower garden around the Hills Hoist and along the side of the driveway, their entire quarter acre was filled with vegetables, cleverly using every space available. The thick-stemmed grapevine used the boundary fence as its support, until the roles reversed. A small concrete path ran directly down the middle of the perfectly manicured garden, with not a weed in sight. The tomatoes stood tall, with thick, flaky-stemmed mānuka posts as their supports for the summer.

The back contained a large lemon tree, where rows of dwarf butter beans grew. I vividly remember sitting down there eating these pretty pastel-yellow beans straight from the patch. I knew exactly what size they had to be for the perfect snack.

A large chest freezer in the shed stored a lot of their produce. There were also countless preserves – bottled peaches, greengages, boysenberries and pears, all bought or picked in season and stored on wonky wooden shelves. I remember bottled spaghetti in tomato sauce (recipe page 104) and beans done the same way.

We often went to 'pick your own' berry farms, where I learnt what a perfectly ripe boysenberry should look like (actually, should feel like). They rarely made it into the container, and have been the unreachable benchmark for bought punnets of berries ever since. Definitely a reason to grow them in your garden, as a sun-warmed, perfectly ripe berry has no comparison.

It wasn't until I travelled to Italy for the first time in my early twenties that all these things finally made sense, like I'd been breathing through a straw and was finally able to take a deep breath. I didn't feel like a tourist; the flavours were exactly what I knew. My world view has been imprinted with these memories and flavours, brought from Italy and reimagined growing up as a Kiwi.

My mother was a trained chef who ran her own café. It was called Eliza's Pantry and was near Kirkcaldie & Stains department store in Wellington. Our school lunches were always full of freshly baked goodies, such as apple cake (page 188), oaty slice (page 66) and coconut loaf (page 201) – recipes I've since riffed on a little to make my own.

My grandparents didn't have a lot, and died when I was still quite young, so their true heirloom was Nonna's recipe book. Its appearance is unassuming, but her handwriting and the threadbare bottom-right corners of some of the pages, slightly gritty with flour, evoke fond memories. Several of the recipes have a name in the top right corner, which is the person the recipe came from. The tomato sauce (page 99) has 'Mum's', so that would be my great-grandmother's recipe … and it's the reason I grow a particular type of tomato still.

Harvesting your own fresh fruit and vegetables brings a whole different level of real flavour to your cooking. Everything is at its peak. I've also come across more new foods through my garden than I have in food stores and, from a culinary perspective, that has been exciting. There is also a thrill, having grown something from seed, to knowing your food is completely free of sprays or chemicals.

My very first recommendation is to start small. If you're a beginner, don't try to start a market garden all in one season; take your time to learn and to grow alongside your plants. Gardening is a year-round thing, so you don't need to wait for spring specifically. There is never a better time to start than when inspiration hits. Choose a plant that likes the season you are in and give it a go. In fact, one plant each month would be an excellent start, as opposed to a big spring splurge on lots and lots of different seedlings.

Rather than sharing outright 'dos and dont's' for each plant, I offer tips I have discovered through years of gardening. But the best way to learn is to get to know your own garden. Notice its details. What kind of birds visit? What grows well in your area? What are people in local groups growing?

Its a wonderful way to be 'in the moment' and slow right down. I have learnt about many of my favourite plants through trial and error. Asparagus and avocado weren't being grown by any of my friends or neighbours, but I did a wee bit of research, put them in, and the results have been astounding. If you start with a perennial, it will add to your permanent garden rather than needing to be replaced each year, and gives you more reward for your effort.

My second piece of advice is to grow what you enjoy eating. There is very little joy in a bumper crop of silverbeet if you don't like to eat it. Growing things you like makes the effort – and yes there is a little required – all the sweeter.

I kept adding to my garden over the decades. I learnt about tomatoes and added beans into the mix, then zucchini and cucumbers, each with their own set of requirements. Just like with cooking, gardening requires a level of curiosity, as the learning is infinite. After all this time I am still learning new tips and tricks

I have things that grow well in my garden and things that do not, and that's okay. Sometimes, depending on how much I like the fruit or vegetable, I will try several different spots or styles of growing to see if I can persuade it to grow.

I always feel the need to explain myself when people visit my garden: the lawn cut on one side of the house and not the other, the flowers or herbs that haven't been completely 'de-headed', nasturtiums sprouting haphazardly around the edges of the vegetable patch. My garden is low maintenance, albeit slightly wild, organic and predominately perennial, with all our favourite seasonal plants thrown in where my time commitments allow.

Food forest, permaculture and organic are the undertones to my gardening style, where the essentially lazy gardener can plant something once, and the fruit or vegetables repeat year after year for very little input. It also means balancing cost and benefit. Sometimes a fruit or veggie in season is so cheap to buy, compared to the effort and space to grow it.

I suppose the word for my garden is 'sustainable', which to me means that I manage my impact on the environment in a simple but profound way. With a full quota of insects and birds, I no longer need to look for remedies to bug-related problems in the garden. It comes down to taking care of the pollinating insects by providing food and habitats for them, and attracting pest-eating birds throughout the year. Those vegetable or flower seedheads become food for the ecosystem, meaning that when you need the bees and pollinating insects they are already in your garden. Providing food for these pollinators out of season is key.

This also means being aware of what you spray in your garden. If you use insecticides, you are also killing or harming your pollinators. One of my philosophies is to instead try and attract wildlife. For example, wax-eye (tauhou) diets include aphids, so researching each pest that you come across and providing its predator with an inviting environment can do wonders for the overall health of your garden – and your family.

Nostrana means 'homegrown' but its meaning is so much more. It also means 'ours': the making (or growing) of something with the intent of sharing it with others. This book is about rekindling the joy of a home garden and kitchen. It is intrinsically satisfying to grow something tasty and either eat it standing there in the garden or to create something delicious with it in the kitchen to share with others. Strawberries are tastier, apples are crunchier, asparagus could be mistaken for snow peas in sweetness, egg yolks are yellower and fresh herbs are perpetually on hand. But it is also a joy to share a bumper harvest with friends. Our busy lives mean that having fresh, flavourful, healthy food straight from the garden can feel like a pipe dream but, taken in small steps, it's simpler than you might think.

This book is a collection of my favourite recipes, created from and inspired by what I have in my own garden, my nonna's recipe book and my mother's café. *Nostrana* is about what I do, where I am from, and who I am. I hope you and yours enjoy it.

TOP LEFT *My ancestral village at the foot of Stromboli, a live volcano, is still just a small scattering of whitewashed villas on a boat-strewn, black-sand beach.*

ABOVE *I still enjoy beans picked fresh from the garden.*

Sweet Peas
Purple & Mauve
Mar 2019
I really like the
size of these
a suburban veg
flower garden
Grow to about
fairly small heads

Spring

GROWING FROM SEED

For new gardeners, growing plants from seed can seem too hard, but there are a few reasons why, for some plants, and your own journey into gardening, this is important.

Some herbs and vegetables do better grown from seed sown directly into the spot where they will live. Often if the plant has a tap root (one long root rather than a lacy network of roots) it will sulk if moved, they don't like that root to be disturbed. Carrots and radishes are a good example of this, but there are also herbs like parsley that benefit from staying in one spot.

If I'm not familiar with a plant, I might do both: plant some seedlings and seeds at the same time. That way I automatically have a staggered planting.

Most of my seedlings grow on my kitchen windowsill, where I can see them every day. This isn't absolutely necessary, as a good sunny spot outside is fine, I just love to see them emerge. It has taught me how to identify what all the different plants look like at a young age – so now when I'm weeding my garden I can tell the difference between plants and weeds in the patch. Often plants self-seed so if you can recognise their seedlings you can leave them be, and have a free harvest coming your way.

The process itself is simple, pop a seed in the dirt, keep it warm and watered, and you will be rewarded. The reality is that you do need to do a little preparation for the best results, but don't be too intimidated by it all. Remember, the simplest weed will grow in the most obscure crack without any assistance, so sometimes too much help is as bad as not enough.

You need to start with fairly fine soil, so the seed isn't hindered by any large lumps. The soil needs to be moist, so sit the pot in a dish of water to let it absorb the water. But don't keep them too moist, as you don't want your seeds to rot. I usually use my own soil and compost, but if you are new to this I would recommend buying a seed-raising mix or fine potting mix, just to make sure you have no bugs or other seeds contend with.

Some plants are much easier and more rewarding to start from seed than others. Beans and tomatoes are my personal favourites from seed, started in the kitchen, and radishes and carrots are best sowed straight into the garden.

Check that you are growing your plants at the right time for the conditions that they are going to like in the garden, particularly if you are starting them indoors, otherwise they will just sulk or die once they get to the garden. We use a process called 'hardening off', whereby the seedlings spend a little time outside each day and then overnight to adjust to the change in temperatures, before they are planted in the garden.

Self-sown plants seem to be much hardier, and grow in conditions where you would never dream of planting a seedling. I have an avocado growing in one compost heap and a banana tree in another, which I will have to do something about! Tomatoes growing wild in my lawn are far less temperamental than the ones I've nurtured, so I really advise keeping the 'volunteer' seedling. Even if you move them to another spot in the garden, they have a toughness about them that is beneficial.

Asparagus

If you can grow a daffodil, you can grow asparagus.

It's been life-changing, growing these little gems in my own garden, and what no one told me was how ridiculously easy they are to grow. I honestly wish that I had started with this vegetable, but unfortunately left it until much later to attempt, because I somehow thought they were difficult to grow. They are not.

They are the 'unicorn' of plants to have in the garden. Planted one time, they return every year. They are an expensive vegetable to buy, but you will have the first and last of the season – before they hit the shops and long after they are gone. Very few bugs or birds bother with them so you don't need to spray or net them. Every day, new ones pop up.

They can be grown from seed or crowns. I would recommend crowns if you can find them, as the wait time to the first full harvest is cut by a year. That said, the hardest part of growing your own asparagus is the wait, as they need a few years before they come into their own and turn out beautiful fat spears.

They are usually found dormant in packets with the flower bulbs, hanging on a stand at large hardware stores or garden centres.

The crown is an octopus-like root system. Once planted, you need to leave the green growth on top for a few years to support the maturing of the root system. As the plant matures and you start to harvest from it, you will still need to let the green growth return at the end of the season, leaving a few stems to turn into giant ferns and die back naturally to nourish the root system.

This means that when you plant them initially you need to choose a spot where they can grow on their own, or reasonably uninterrupted, for their life span, which could be up to 20 years. I have moved my asparagus from one bed to another and they did sulk for a while, but then leapt back to life, so it's not set in stone. Everything I have read and done, up until this year, says that they need to be on their own, but this year I planted strawberries and cucumber among them, kind of as a permaculture/food forest theory. So far they are all thriving. The asparagus have deep roots, while the strawberries have shallow roots, but they prefer the same conditions. The asparagus has even protected the strawberries from birds. The cucumbers were planted as I let the asparagus grow tall for the end of the season, and are now happily using the asparagus stems as a natural trellis. Everyone, including me, is very happy.

To prepare your garden, choose a reasonably well drained site, or create a raised area for them using plenty of compost and manure. Sit each crown on top of a small mound of dirt, so all the individual roots flow down the side. Cover with an inch or so of soil (as you would any other bulb), so that the top of the plant is 'just' below the soil. Layer the top with some straw or other mulch. I have even used garden leaf litter in the past.

When spring arrives the first little spears will pop through. For the first two years or so they will be quite slim, so leave them to grow into ferns, as this will feed and strengthen the roots. They will grow quite tall, and by winter they will have turned brown and died back. At this point trim the stems back to about 3–4cm above the soil level, and mulch well. This needs to be done every year, so at the end of every picking season, or if the new spears start to become quite slim, leave them at this point. By about the third year the spears should be quite a lot fatter, and worth picking.

Very few pests or diseases bother asparagus, so they are a welcome addition to an organic garden, as a problem-free spring vegetable.

RECIPES

Asparagus & Lemon Ricotta Ravioli

SERVES 4

RAVIOLI
Pasta dough (see page 239), or use
    wonton wrappers (see note)
2 cups chopped asparagus
1 cup (120g) peas
1 cup (240g) ricotta (see page 230)
½ cup (40g) grated parmesan
1 tsp finely grated lemon zest

GARLIC BUTTER SAUCE
75g butter
⅓ cup (50g) pine nuts
2 garlic cloves, finely chopped
½ cup chopped perpetual spinach
Lemon juice, to taste
Fresh watercress or rocket, to serve

This is such a 'beginning of spring' dish for me. The asparagus spears pop up in the garden a few at a time, so this recipe makes them go a little further. The milk I make the ricotta with starts to become a little richer and creamier, so this is a very representative dish of early spring.

Make the pasta dough, following the recipe on page 239.

While the dough rests, make the filling. Cook the asparagus and peas in salted boiling water for 3–4 minutes, until tender. Drain well then puree to your preferred consistency – I like a little texture. Set aside to cool, then mix in the ricotta, parmesan and lemon zest. Season with salt and pepper to taste.

Cut dough into 8 pieces. Roll dough through the pasta machine, following the recipe and finishing on the third- or second-last setting, until you have 8 long, thin sheets.

Place heaped teaspoons of filling along the length of one sheet, leaving about 4cm between mounds and from the edge of the dough. Gently drape a second sheet of dough over the top and press around each mound, removing any air pockets as you go.

Repeat with remaining dough and filling. Cut each ravioli into squares and place on a lightly floured (or baking paper lined) tray.

For the sauce, heat the butter in a large frying pan until it foams, add the pine nuts and cook until golden. Add the garlic and cook, stirring, until soft and lightly golden. Add the spinach and squeeze of lemon juice. Remove from the heat and set aside until the ravioli is ready.

Bring a large pot of salted water to the boil, then reduce to a simmer. Cook the ravioli in batches for 2–3 minutes, until tender. Reheat the sauce. Use a slotted spoon to transfer the ravioli to the sauce.

Serve with fresh watercress or rocket.

NOTE: I always keep wonton wrappers on hand to make quick ravioli, without having to bust out the pasta-making gear.

Grilled Asparagus with Anchovy Dressing

SERVES 4

Large handful of asparagus spears,
    trimmed (about 20 spears)
Olive oil, for cooking
½ lemon, for grilling

ANCHOVY DRESSING
¼ cup (60ml) lemon juice
3 tbsp olive oil
1 tbsp white vinegar
5 anchovy fillets
1 garlic clove

This is the perfect BBQ dish. The dressing on this dish has more impact on homegrown asparagus, which is profoundly sweeter than anything bought. The taste is more like a sugar snap pea, so this sweet and savoury combination is more pronounced. The dressing needs a light hand and is like using squeeze of lemon juice to highlight the other flavours.

To make the dressing, blend the ingredients to a paste. Adjust the thickness with extra olive oil, if you like. Season with salt and pepper to taste.

For the asparagus, lightly brush the spears with oil and cook on a hot BBQ grill until lightly charred. While grilling, add halved lemon to the grill pan.

Served slightly warm, with the dressing drizzled over and halved lemon on the side.

NOTE: This dish is made more vibrant with the addition of garnishes such as soft-boiled eggs, olives, lemon rind and a crumble of ricotta.

Asparagus, Pea & Parmesan Custard Tarts

MAKES 6

300g shortcrust pastry
2 cups (500ml) cream
1 cup (250ml) milk
120g parmesan, finely grated
5 egg yolks
Pinch of smoked paprika
6 asparagus spears
1 cup (120g) fresh or frozen peas
Pea shoots, shaved parmesan and
    lemon zest, to garnish
Lemon juice, verjuice (see page
    234) or balsamic vinegar, to
    drizzle

I can never grow enough peas for our household – we literally eat kilos of them. The thought of surrendering that much space in my garden to be self-sufficient in peas seems a bit much when frozen peas are actually good value. I do grow some along the edges of my planter boxes, so that they tumble down the sides (rather than up little trellises). When I do grow peas and snow peas I like to use them in recipes that really hero them as 'fresh from the garden stars', rather than just being a side dish.

•

Preheat the oven to 180°C fan-forced. Roll the pastry out to about 5mm thickness. Cut 6 discs from the pastry and use to line 6 individual pie or tart dishes, 10–12cm across the top and about 2cm deep.

Refrigerate for at least 10 minutes (longer is fine). Place dishes onto a large baking tray. Place a square of baking paper over the pastry and fill with baking weights. Bake for 10 minutes then remove weights and paper and cook a further 5 minutes, until lightly golden. Set aside. Reduce oven to 150°C.

Mix the cream, milk and grated parmesan in a heatproof bowl. Place it on a pan of simmering water to heat gently until the parmesan melts into the cream and milk (do not let it boil). Remove bowl from the heat and set aside to cool.

Whisk in the egg yolks with the smoked paprika and season with a little salt and pepper. Pour the mixture into the cooled pastry cases. Bake for 12–15 minutes, until just set but still slightly wobbly. Set aside to cool.

Slice the asparagus spears thinly lengthwise. Briefly blanch in boiling water for a moment and then refresh in iced water. Drain and lightly shake dry. Repeat with the peas. Arrange asparagus and peas onto tarts, and garnish with pea shoots, shaved parmesan and lemon zest. Drizzle lightly with lemon juice, verjuice or balsamic vinegar.

Asparagus & Goats Cheese Pasta Bake

SERVES 4

500g asparagus, woody ends
    removed
5 sprigs thyme
300g fusilli pasta (or any
    preferred shape)
50g butter
1 onion, finely diced
⅓ cup (50g) plain flour
2½ cups (625ml) milk
1 cup (250ml) cream
2 cloves garlic, minced
150g goats cheese
1½ cups (100g) breadcrumbs
2 tbsp olive oil
25g pine nuts
Lemon zest, for garnish

This is my spring garden take on the classic mac 'n' cheese. The first asparagus that peep through (or that appear at the market) need to be celebrated, and this recipe turns those first few bundles into an entire meal. If you want to make this dish in two portions, it's perfect for freezing for another time – just pop it in the freezer instead of baking it, and extend the baking time by about 10 minutes if you bake from frozen.

•

Preheat the oven to 180°C. Grease a large (35cm × 20cm) baking dish. Slice asparagus on a slight diagonal into roughly 2cm slices, reserving some of the tops for garnish. Strip the leaves from the thyme sprigs.

Bring a pot of water to the boil, lower to a simmer then add a little salt and pasta. Cook pasta for half the time indicted on packet directions. Drain pasta and tip into the bottom of the baking dish.

While the water is boiling, heat the butter in a large pan, add the onion and cook until translucent (about 5 minutes), stirring occasionally. Add the flour to the onion and stir until you have a paste. Mix milk and cream together then, using a whisk, add them slowly to the pan, whisking continuously. Simmer for a minute, then stir in the garlic, asparagus and thyme. Simmer another minute then turn off the heat and crumble in the goats cheese. Season with salt and pepper, to taste. Stir to combine and then pour over the pasta, and stir through gently until evenly mixed.

Mix the breadcrumbs with the olive oil and then spread evenly over the top. Decorate with the asparagus tips and pine nuts. Bake for 20 minutes, or until the top is a lovely golden colour.

Add the lemon zest and serve while warm.

Salad Leaves

This has become a large category in my garden, because of the variation of what I like to use in a salad. Because they are such quick crops, I often use them as little gap fillers between seasons, or until I need the space in the main garden. I often sow these around crops that take a long time to germinate or grow, so that I make use of the space and also block out any weeds from taking hold.

I usually buy these as seeds (or leave a previous plant to go to seed naturally) and their versatility in where I can grow them is vast. I have a half-wine barrel by my back door (I call it the 'picking barrel') that is home to salad leaves that I can grab without actually going to the garden. It's great to be able to just pick a few leaves as I need them without harvesting a whole plant. For a quick sandwich filling or handful of rocket or basil for garnish, this is my go-to spot.

The barrel also contains a permanent celery plant and carrot, both of which are several years old now and have been treated like perennials. I just constantly pick the leaves without disturbing the root. The same can be done with a beetroot plant. These will survive winter a little better than traditional lettuce varieties and are a little less attractive to slugs.

More substantial offerings are grown down in the main vegetable patch. I've become far broader in what I categorise as 'salad' leaves – nasturtium, mint, sorrel, lemon balm and even edible flowers feature in coleslaws and leafy salads now. My salads have gone from an everyday side dish to a really vibrant, flavour-popping event. (And see the petal sugars recipe on page 56.)

Successfully growing salad leaves takes a fairly simple formula of sunshine and water. Not too much sunshine, however. Spring is their favourite season, as summer can be a bit too hot – so some afternoon shade at this time of year is good. Then there is the added challenge of slugs, bugs and birds enjoying a snack.

If summer gets too hot and they run short of water, the plants will bolt (go to seed quickly). When this happens you will notice a white sap when you pick the leaves. This means that they are going to be a little bitter to taste. In summer you need a well-mulched, shady spot for plants with tender leaves. My recommendation is to have a couple of areas that you rotate naturally.

Snails are their biggest enemy. One bite on the stem of a tiny young seedling and it's all over! There are lots of methods for controlling these pests – I go out at night and collect them to feed to the chickens. Another way is to make the soil around the seedlings unpleasant for snails or slugs to crawl across. You can use crushed eggshells, sand or salt on the edges of your garden. Beer traps are another organic solution. Put some beer in a shallow dish in the garden. The snails will congregate on the dish, making it easy to dispose of a good number of them at one time. I haven't had great success with many of these methods. I generally cover my plants until they are big enough to handle a snail assault. Birds will also have a snack on your leaves – so if you notice little beak-shaped bites in the ends of your leaves, that's likely a bird.

Perpetual Spinach

Strictly speaking this is probably closer to the beet or chard family, but in kitchen terms it is my spinach replacement to cook with.

It can be used both raw and cooked, and it behaves and tastes exactly like spinach, so it is an amazing alternative to true spinach. The stem is tougher than true spinach, so I usually cut it out (like I would with chard). It is edible, however, so I slice it finely and cook it separately to the leaf, with the help of a little garlic and butter. The other thing to do with the stem is a quick pickle, and it's a brilliant thing to have on hand in the fridge.

The ease and speed of growing perpetual spinach will be what really wins you over. Once planted it is quite prolific and will keep producing leaves all year. It is definitely not fussy about the soil. It grows in wherever the seed has landed, which is often the garden path and cracks in the planter boxes, like a tough little weed would. I often move them while they are little to a spot with more room for them to really flourish. They are a tap root plant, so they don't like being moved much, but doing it while they are quite small seems to have the best success. Based on this I would recommend planting seeds directly, rather than seedlings. If you buy seedlings, just give them a little extra water and care until they get going. They often sit for a while, sulking about being moved, before they burst into life.

I plant several patches of perpetual spinach in various places in the garden, so that they grow at different rates. Rather than lots of leaves at once, I pick a few of the larger outer leaves off the biggest plants, and leave the inner leaves to grow a little more. This is where the 'perpetual' comes in – the more you pick from the outer leaves, the more new leaves it seems to grow in the centre. Finally it will run to seed, but even then the leaves are still lovely to eat – they don't turn bitter or tough the way a lettuce does. If left completely, it will regrow the next spring. I tend to pull them out

because all the seeds that have self-sown germinate really well.

Not much bothers the plants in the way of pests or disease; even the birds leave them alone. This makes perpetual spinach a great addition to the organic garden, as there is no need for sprays, which means less work and less worrying about any residual chemicals.

I leave at least one plant to self-seed each season and as a result haven't bought new plants, or grown seeds to plant out, in years. Those one or two plants do the work for me! They supply me with greens all through winter, and summer if I water them regularly, although by spring I'm ready for some new flavours!

Originally, I had so much I would freeze batches of spinach, blanched and squeezed out, but I simply don't bother taking up the freezer space any more. I often just sneak a little into recipes that can manage a little hidden spinach.

RECIPES

Fregola with Spinach & Feta

1¼ cups (210g) fregola
2 tbsp olive oil
30g butter
2 garlic cloves, crushed
1 spring onion, chopped
Pinch of dried chilli flakes
250g blanched or thawed frozen
    spinach, squeezed dry and
    roughly chopped
100g feta, crumbled
1 tsp finely grated lemon zest

Fregola is interchangeable to Israeli couscous, acini di pepe or risoni, which are all very small types of pasta. It makes a lovely side dish for a summer meal, but is just as good as a 'take to work' lunch.

•

Cook the fregola in a large pot of well salted boiling water according to packet directions or until 'al dente'. Drain well, cover and set aside.

Heat the oil and butter in a large frying pan over medium heat. Add the garlic, spring onion and chilli flakes and cook until just soft. Add the spinach and cook, tossing, until heated through and the ingredients are evenly combined.

Add fregola to the pan and toss to combine, then toss through the feta and lemon zest. Season with salt and pepper to taste.

All the Greens Ricotta Tart

50g butter
1 garlic clove, finely chopped
2 cups trimmed and sliced
 vegetables (see note)
3 cups chopped perpetual spinach
3 eggs
¼ cup (60ml) cream
150g ricotta, crumbled
 (see page 230)
100g parmesan, finely grated
3 tbsp pesto (any of the recipes on
 pages 54–5)
2 tbsp finely chopped soft fresh
 herbs (such as parsley, oregano,
 sage or coriander)
6 sheets filo pastry

Sometimes the garden gives a little bit of many things – this is a good way to turn it all into a delicious dish.

•

Preheat the oven to 190°C fan-forced. Lightly grease a 20cm (top measurement) pie dish.

Melt half the butter in a large frying pan over medium heat. Add the garlic then the vegetables and spinach. Cook gently until just tender. Set aside to cool.

Whisk the eggs and cream together in a large bowl. Gently mix in the cooled vegetables and then the ricotta, parmesan, pesto and herbs until just combined. Season with salt and pepper.

Melt the remaining butter and use to brush onto the filo sheets. Stack together and line the pie dish with the filo.

Pour in the filling, then either trim the extra filo, or (like me) scrunch the edges over a little, around the rim of the pie dish. Brush with any remaining butter

Bake for 40 minutes, until filling has set and pastry is golden. Serve hot or at room temperature.

•

NOTE: Use any vegetables you have, such as zucchini, asparagus, carrot or leek.

Southern Italian Spinach

SERVES 2 AS A SIDE

2 tbsp olive oil
2 garlic cloves, finely chopped
1 small onion, finely chopped
⅓ cup (55g) sultanas
¼ cup (60ml) white wine
350g perpetual spinach, thick
    stems removed
⅓ cup (50g) pine nuts, toasted
Finely grated lemon zest, to taste

Heat a large frying pan over medium heat. Add the olive oil, then garlic and onion, and cook until translucent. Add the sultanas and white wine, and when the liquid is almost all absorbed add the spinach and then the pine nuts.

Cook, stirring, until the spinach has wilted. Remove from the heat and add the lemon zest. Season with salt and pepper to taste.

Korean-style Spinach

SERVES 2 AS A SIDE

350g perpetual spinach, thick
    stems removed
1 garlic clove, crushed
2 tsp soy sauce
1 tsp sesame oil
2 tsp sesame seeds
Chilli, if desired

Briefly blanch the spinach in boiling water until wilted. Drain then plunge into bowl of iced water. Drain well and squeeze out the excess water.

Mix the remaining ingredients in a large bowl, then add the drained spinach and toss through to coat completely.

Spinach Crackle

1 tsp finely chopped fresh chilli
1 tsp finely chopped fresh ginger
1 tsp finely chopped fresh garlic
1 shallot or small onion, finely
　　sliced
Olive oil, to shallow-fry
10 perpetual spinach leaves,
　　finely sliced
1 tsp sesame seeds

Combine the chilli, ginger, garlic and shallot in a heatproof bowl.

Heat the oil in a pan or wok over medium-high heat. When it is hot, drop the spinach in and cook for a minute, until crispy. Use a slotted spoon to transfer to a plate lined with paper towel.

Ladle a little of the oil into the bowl with the chilli mixture and let it sizzle. Drain through a wire sieve to remove the oil. Add the mixture to the spinach and toss to combine, then toss the sesame seeds through.

This is great just to snack on, or sprinkled on top of a salad or cooked veggies to add a crispy texture.

Sauteed Spinach with Feta & Roasted Garlic

SERVES 6

1 whole garlic bulb
2 tbsp olive oil
350g perpetual spinach, thick
　　stems removed
¼ cup (60g) crème fraiche
100g feta
Handful of parsley, roughly
　　chopped
Finely grated lemon zest, to taste

Preheat the oven to 190°C fan-forced.

Cut the garlic bulb in half horizontally. Place cut side up into a shallow baking dish and drizzle with a little of the olive oil. Roast for about 20 minutes, until soft. This can be done ahead of time if you prefer.

Heat the remaining oil in a deep frying pan over medium heat. Add the spinach and crème fraiche and cook, tossing constantly, until the spinach has wilted. Transfer to a large bowl to cool.

Mix with crumbled feta, roasted garlic (squeezed from the skin), parsley and lemon zest. Season with pepper if you like.

Radishes & Carrots

The ultimate gourmet vegetables for beginners. They are easy to grow from seed and quick to mature. Succession planting and seed saving are a breeze. They are edible at every stage, from micro greens to root, flower, seedhead and even the seeds.

The soil that you plant them in needs to be free of obstructions that cause the root to divide or stop. They will do well in planter pots on your deck for this reason, or in rows alongside each other in the veggie patch, as markers for each other. The radish will be ready first and be gone by the time the carrots start to get bigger – so it's a good use of space. Simply plant a row of seeds every week or so, rather than everything at once, to ensure you have an ongoing supply of snacks.

While you only ever see one or two types in the shops, the variety of colours, shapes and flavour profiles available as seeds are endless. Carrots are one of those vegetables that become quite cheap to buy in the supermarket at times during the year, so I grow an heirloom white carrot for a bit of variety.

They like the sunshine and can deal with dappled shade, and while they both will grow in most soils, they do benefit from a well composted patch.

You may have heard people talk about 'thinning' carrots – as carrot seeds are very small, it's easy to have them grow too close together. To give a carrot room to grow to full size, you may need to remove some of the others around it. Some gardeners do this early on; I tend to run the gauntlet a little and let them grow to baby carrot size before I remove any, so that I can have a mini feast of roasted baby carrots when I do.

Their main predator is the garden slug, who will take a bite of the bulb, but nothing too serious. I've also learnt the hard way to protect them from the blackbirds and doves ferreting around in my garden, who will scatter the seeds and seedlings across the yard. The result of these overfed birds is a healthy crop of root vegetables growing in my lawn. The plants often have their tops mown off but their roots will fatten. I now strategically place a rock near any I spot, to ensure they aren't run over too many times!

While carrots are happily left in the ground until you need them, radishes need to be picked before they get too big and woody. If this happens, just leave them where they are and let them go to seed. Save the seeds, or even pop a few of their seed pods in your next salad – just as enjoyable as the root itself.

RECIPES

Lime-pickled Radish

1 bunch radishes (about 8–10),
    thinly sliced
1 small red onion, sliced
Few sprigs of thyme
½ cup (125ml) lime juice
¼ cup (60ml) water
2 tbsp sugar
½ tsp salt

Radishes are great candidates for any kind of quick pickle recipe. In no time at all you will have a jar of pickles on hand to add to any meals or platters. This is one of my favourites, because I often have really ripe sweet limes and radishes ready in the garden at the same time.

Pickled radish provides a lovely crisp, crunchy, sweet-and-sour pop of flavour to any dish that is a fresher and brighter replacement for more traditional pickles like gherkins, onions or piccalilli. Use these on tacos, burgers, sandwiches, atop a salad, as thin slivers in sushi or on a charcuterie board.

•

Pack the radishes, onion and thyme into a sterilised jar (see page 249).

Combine the lime juice, water, sugar and salt in a small saucepan and bring to the boil. Pour the hot liquid into the jar. Put the lid on and leave to cool on the counter.

Once cool, store in the fridge for up to 4 weeks. These are best served chilled.

Fresh Butter-dipped Radishes

8–10 baby radishes (or 4–5 larger
   ones cut in half)
Sea salt

CULTURED BUTTER
1 litre full cream milk
2 tbsp buttermilk
½ tsp fine sea salt

*A good-quality butter is a real treat, especially on freshly baked bread
or scones. I often make cultured butter for slathering onto and dunking
into anything I'm going to devour directly. This delicious little combo is
basically compulsory to make with a fresh batch of butter.*

•

To make cultured butter, combine the milks in a large bowl and
leave in a warm place for 12–24 hours (the longer left, the better
the flavour).

Chill in the fridge for 30 minutes, then use an electric beater to
whisk until it thickens then separates. A thick ball of butter will form,
as well as a thin cloudy liquid sometimes referred to as whey. This
can be poured off and kept chilled for other uses such as pancakes
or baking.

Rinse ball of butter under chilled water, until the water runs
clear. Mix salt through gently and form into the required shape or
place in butter dish (see page 47 for herb butter options). Chill
until required.

To dip the radishes, line a plate or board with greaseproof paper.

Hold each radish by its stem and dip in soft (but not melted)
cultured butter.

Sprinkle with sea salt.

Let chill for a moment or two in the fridge. Best served chilled.

•

NOTE: Substitute baby carrots for a sweeter alternative. If you prefer
regular butter, you can omit the buttermilk and whisk full cream
milk straight from the fridge.

Herbs

Herbs are the best-value plants to grow. They are expensive to buy, don't last long in the fridge and you often only need small quantities, so end up with a lot of waste. Growing your own herbs will save you money and give you a lot of satisfaction – adding even one thing from your garden to a meal is so much fun, and can start a gardening addiction! My standard advice for growing herbs is to start with a few of your favourites and try to match them to areas in your garden that they might like. You will learn as you go, as they all have different preferences and personalities, and can have vastly different growing requirements.

Mediterranean-style herbs, such as sage, lavender, rosemary, oregano and thyme enjoy the heat and will happily grow in conditions other plants may not tolerate. The hottest corner of my garden with sometimes the worst soil has seen some of these guys thrive. It is a brilliant way of disguising a 'tough' corner of the garden and making it look lush.

Parsley, coriander and mint like the early spring conditions, good soil, water and sunshine, and not too much heat.

A good tip is to take a little walk around your neighbourhood and see what is going well in other people's gardens, and then just go ahead and plant some and see how they go. I actually recommend this as the best way to get an understanding of gardening in general. It's a lot like cooking – you will have some failures along the way, but actually doing it is the best way to learn.

Some herbs are perennial and others are annual. I don't specifically have a 'herb garden'. The plants are scattered throughout my garden, so that they are in areas that they prefer. In some instances they are carrying out a task, such as working as a live mulch base or hedging, depending on their growing style. My thyme is a ground cover in a little BBQ area garden box, attracting the bees and providing some relief from the sun hitting the soil for other plants, as well as the obvious kitchen provisions it provides. The rosemary is a live hedge and bee attractant. You can see how, if carefully thought through, you can have your herbs playing double duty in a lot of areas of the garden.

There are lots of categories you can choose for your herbs. Mine is purely culinary, but you may choose a medicinal theme, or herbs for making teas, or just for attracting butterflies and bees. They could be for scent or sensory reasons – it is fun to have a theme and start a collection that way. I started a 'chicken's favourites' when the girls first arrived. I found that nasturtiums and lemon balm were good for them to eat, and would put things like lavender in their nesting boxes. You could consider your household pets when you choose herbs and include ones that they like or are good for them.

It took me a while to really start to use the herbs in my garden and I would often remember at the last minute that I had this resource, dashing to the garden mid-cooking. My top cooking tip is to tour the garden one evening and pick a handful of different herbs to sit on your kitchen bench in a jar of water, to add to your meals throughout the week. Just adding a few chopped fresh herbs at the end of cooking can lift any dish to another level, both flavour-wise and visually.

USING HERBS

USING HERBS

Drying herbs is a great way to preserve them. You can tie them in little bundles and hang them upside down in a warm dry place, or spread them out on a baking tray and leave overnight in the oven with residual heat from baking. Thyme, bay, mint, marjoram, tarragon, rosemary, sage and even citrus peel do well with this method.

These are some of my other favourite ways to use herbs:

Bouquet garni

This is a little bundle of fresh or dry herbs that is added to stocks, sauces and soups and removed at the end of cooking. You can enclose them in a little cheesecloth or muslin pouch, but I like to just tie them with kitchen string. That way I can just put it into the compost after it has been removed from the pan. A traditional bouquet garni consists of bay leaves, parsley stalks and thyme sprigs, but you could add other herbs such as chervil or tarragon.

Herb salt

Finely chop (or blitz in a food processor) about 2 cups herb leaves (I like rosemary or sage, or even lemon rind or celery leaves). Combine with ½ cup salt (fine rather than coarse) then spread onto a tray in a very thin layer. Leave in a sunny spot for a few hours until dry. Store in an airtight container.

Bath time

Add a few leaves and flowers of lavender next time you run a bath. Makrut lime peels are my favourite for this, but different herbs have different benefits, so experiment!

Fragrance

To make your house smell divine or to lower anxiety levels, make a simmer pot. Add a handful of rosemary leaves with some lemon zest to a saucepan of water and gently simmer. Cinnamon sticks, and vanilla pods are also great additions.

Freeze to preserve

Pack chopped herbs into ice cube trays and top up with oil. Keep in the freezer and use directly from frozen when cooking. This is best for herbs that you want to cook with, rather than use fresh. These can be individual herbs, or combinations that you use frequently.

Herb oil

Basil oil is the best alternative to pesto and a quick drizzle over tomatoes or cheese toasties is bliss. Blitz basil, garlic cloves, a pinch of salt and a pinch of chilli flakes in the blender, then add olive oil and blitz again. This will keep for a week in the fridge.

Herb butter

Mixing flavours into butters is a lovely way to infuse flavours into something in a luscious way – on top of hot vegetables or mash, rubbed into chicken, or left to melt over a grilled fish or steak. Some of my favourite combinations are cayenne and cumin, dill and lemon, and parsley and capers. To make, soften a large batch of cultured butter (see page 43) and divide into several smaller amounts, blending each with your preference of chopped herbs and ground spices. Using dried ingredients will extend your butter's shelf life. Roll into tubes and store in the freezer. Just take a slice as needed.

Other herb ideas

To elevate any crumbed food, add chopped herbs to the breadcrumbs.

See the Syrups section (page 260) for herb syrup ideas, and the Marinades section for Chimichurri (page 259).

Savoury Herb Shortbread

MAKES 12

1¼ cups (185g) plain flour
2 tbsp chopped sage (or herb
   of choice)
1 cup (80g) finely grated parmesan
Pinch each of salt and cracked
   pepper
120g butter, cut into small cubes
Extra herbs, for decorating
   (optional)

These are ridiculously moreish, so double the recipe if you like. They make a nice change from a sweet biscuit in the afternoon, and are great at aperitivo time!

•

Preheat the oven to 180°C fan-forced and line a large baking tray with baking paper.

Combine all the ingredients except the butter in a food processor and process briefly to combine. Add the butter a few pieces at a time and using the pulse button process briefly between each addition. Once all the butter has been added, process in short bursts until the dough just comes together.

Turn out and gather dough into a ball. Roll into a log about 12cm long and wrap in baking paper. Chill for 10 minutes, then cut into 1cm thick slices.

If you want to decorate with herb leaves, press one gently into the top of each slice. Bake for 10–15 minutes, until they are just pale golden in colour. Leave to cool on the tray, then store in an airtight container.

Herb & Parmesan Savoury French Toast

2 eggs

2 tbsp milk

¼ cup (20g) finely grated
    parmesan

1 tbsp finely chopped fresh thyme

1 tbsp finely chopped sage

1 tbsp finely chopped parsley

1 tbsp finely chopped oregano

2 thick slices of bread
    (sourdough is perfect)

Butter, for cooking

Lightly grilled tomato, labneh
    (or sour cream) and fresh herbs,
    for serving

This recipe is a good way to use up slightly stale bread. Feel free to substitute herbs that you prefer, or have available in your garden. My favourite version of this is to cut a hole in the middle of the bread, prior to 'dipping', then once you have it in the pan and one side is nearly done, add an egg into the middle, let it cook just a little, then flip it. Cutting into this cheesy herby bread and having egg yolk run through takes it to another level.

Whisk the eggs and milk together in a shallow dish, and then stir in the parmesan and herbs. Season with salt and pepper.

Dip the bread in the mixture, turning until it is well coated. Melt the butter in a frying pan over medium-high heat and add the bread. Reduce the heat to medium and cook for a couple of minutes each side, until egg is cooked and golden brown.

I like to serve with a lightly grilled tomato, a dollop of labneh (or sour cream) and a sprinkle of fresh herbs.

Herb Fritto Misto

Selection of herbs
3 eggs
⅓ cup (50g) plain flour
Pinch of salt
½ cup (125ml) milk
Vegetable oil, for frying

This is the ultimate 'whip around the garden' summer meal. I usually use all kinds of herbs: sage, wild onion flower heads, kale, fennel fronds, borage flower, dandelion and so on. But you can also increase the batter quantity if you want to include vegetables as well. Sometimes even lemons are thinly sliced and battered with the other ingredients.

•

Wash and carefully dry herbs. Slice them into even portions if necessary.

Whisk eggs in a large mixing bowl. Gradually whisk in the flour and salt, then slowly add milk while whisking. Leave in the fridge until ready.

Submerge herbs in batter for at least 20 minutes.

Heat oil in deep-edged frying pan until sizzling hot and batch fry the battered herbs until golden brown. Drain on paper towels, and place on a tray in a slightly warm oven while the remaining ingredients are fried.

Sprinkle with salt and serve.

•

NOTE: This recipe works just as well with vegetables gathered from the garden, including thinly sliced lemons! If preparing vegetables, double the batter and use two bowls to avoid the herbs getting lost in a larger bowl.

Pesto

Pesto used to be just basil, but really there are so many combinations that are inspired by fresh garden greens and herbs, and they are so simple to make. Just a few steps to follow and you can have your own garden-inspired pesto that is personal to you. The general theme is a herb or leaf, and a nut (and the range is vast – think walnuts, pine nuts, almonds or pistachios). The olive oil can even be swapped for walnut, avocado or macadamia oil.

If your choice of herb is pungently strong, use a little less and make up the difference with a vibrant green such as spinach, parsley, kale, watercress, or even carrot tops.

For the true blue 'pesto', I usually take a stem or two of basil into the kitchen and remove the leaves that I need, placing the remaining stem in a glass of water. Within days it will have a new set of roots, ready to pop back out in the garden as a new plant – I do this throughout summer and without any effort or money spent have an endless supply of basil

Basil Pesto

2 cups basil leaves, firmly packed
¼ cup (40g) pine nuts, lightly toasted
½ cup (40g) finely grated parmesan
2 garlic cloves
½ cup (125ml) olive oil
Lemon juice or finely grated zest, to taste

Place all the ingredients (except the oil and lemon) into the blender and blitz until well chopped. With the motor running, gradually add the oil until the consistency is smooth.

Season with salt and pepper and a little lemon juice or zest to taste.

Store in an airtight container in the fridge (or the freezer if you have some spare).

Radish Greens Pesto

2 cups roughly chopped radish tops
¼ cup (40g) cashews, lightly toasted
½ cup (40g) finely grated parmesan
2 garlic cloves
¼ cup (60ml) olive oil
Lemon juice or finely grated lemon zest, to taste

Place all the ingredients (except the oil and lemon) into the blender and blitz until well chopped. With the motor running, gradually add the oil until the consistency is smooth.

Season with salt and pepper and a little lemon juice or zest to taste.

Store in an airtight container in the fridge (or the freezer if you have some spare).

Kale Pesto

20 kale leaves (or so)
1 bunch basil (more if you prefer)
½ cup (80g) walnuts, lightly
    toasted
3 garlic cloves
1 cup (250ml) olive oil
Lemon juice or finely grated zest,
    to taste

Place all the ingredients (except the oil and lemon) into the blender and blitz until well chopped. With the motor running, gradually add the oil until the consistency is smooth.

Season with salt and pepper and a little lemon juice or zest to taste.

Store in an airtight container in the fridge (or the freezer if you have some spare).

Parsley & Anchovy Pesto

1 cup flat-leaf parsley leaves
5 anchovy fillets
2 garlic cloves
¼ cup (60ml) olive oil
¼ cup (20g) finely grated pecorino
2 tbsp pine nuts
1 tbsp lemon juice

Blend the parsley, anchovies, garlic and oil until you have a fine paste. Add the pecorino, pine nuts and lemon juice, and blitz briefly – to keep a little of the texture. Add a little more oil if you think it needs it. Season with salt and pepper to taste, but remember the anchovies will add saltiness.

OTHER PESTO COMBINATIONS

Mint & toasted sunflower seeds

Coriander & walnuts

Sundried tomatoes & pine nuts

Rocket & cashews

Carrot tops & toasted macadamias

Petal Sugars

VARIED

White sugar
Flower petals
    Blue Sugar – use cornflower
    Red Sugar – use pōhutakawa
    Yellow Sugar – use calendula

This is a brilliant (literally) use of edible garden flowers. I use these for sprinkling on cupcakes or cakes, on the rim of a cocktail glass – anywhere I might use sprinkles or edible glitter. The ones that I have chosen to share are the colours that I have found last the longest in the pantry. The colours mute after a few months, but still have wonderful hues to them. To try other flowers, first make sure they are edible, then test them to see if they hold their colours by drying a few petals (left out on a plate, or in a flower press). Some aren't very good and will just turn brown, so avoid those. Others will dry perfectly, holding their colours.

•

Making just one colour at a time, choose your petals, fresh from the garden. For every ½ cup of petals, use ½ cup white sugar.

Put petals and sugar in a blender and blitz in short bursts (just a second at a time), until you have the consistency that you want. I like mine quite fine, so that you wouldn't know that it contains petals.

Line a small tray or dish with baking paper and spread the mixture out in a fine layer. Leave in a warm place to dry.

After a day or two transfer to a clean, dry airtight jar. The mixture will clump together as it dries, so gently separate as you put it in the jar. If dried fully you can store these indefinitely.

Strawberries

Strawberries are very easy to grow and perfect for balcony pots, garden edging or as an entire lush patch in your garden.

They literally live on water and sunshine, but the key to an impressive harvest is a good layer of compost or manure underneath them. A layer of straw in between the plants for the fruit to rest on as it ripens helps prevent any fungal problems. If you live in a particularly cold climate, cover the entire plant with straw for winter.

Strawberries don't have many pests to watch out for, which is what makes them such a great low-key addition to the garden. Once they start to ripen you may need to cover your plant with netting, a wire cloche (upside down wire rubbish bin in my case) or even an old glass jar. This will stop the birds from devouring them. The berries won't ripen much after picking, so allowing them to fully ripen on the plant is best.

When runners appear early on in the season it pays to pick them off. This will direct growth toward the strawberries. Later on in the season you can decide whether you would like to grow a new plant from the runners or continue to pick them off.

To grow another plant, pin the new leaves on the runner into the soil, by placing a small stone on top of the runner near the leaves. Once it has formed roots simply cut the stem from the parent plant. It can then be transferred to another spot or left to replace the parent plant in the future. Alternatively, you could pot them up and make them a gift to another strawberry lover!

The productive lifespan of a strawberry plant is several years. After about three or four years, they will still produce strawberries, but they will be far less plentiful. This is where it pays to have collected the runners or replaced the strawberry plants with bought new ones.

As the outer leaves of the strawberry age and start to turn yellow and brown, remove and dispose of them.

As my first strawberries ripen, I will often devour them, sunshine-warm, in the garden. My ways of dealing with 'just a few' have sharpened over the years. Freezing berries is the best way to keep them to cook with and I have provided a few recipes that use frozen strawberries. Especially if you have a smaller garden, you can just pick a few at a time as they ripen then add to an airtight container in the freezer until you have enough to work with. Just remove the hulls before freezing.

They can be used easily in so many recipes later on, or simply dropped into smoothies or blended with icing sugar for a quick coulis.

Strawberries & Cream

To elevate strawberries without too much fussing, simply slice or dice 8 berries and toss with 1 tbsp honey, 1 tsp balsamic vinegar and a pinch of sea salt. Leave for at least 30 minutes (or in the fridge overnight) to become syrupy. You could even just use 2 tsp caster sugar, if you prefer. Serve on porridge, pancakes or waffles, with mascarpone (see page 232).

Strawberry & Goats Cheese Gelato

6 cups (about 800g) frozen
    strawberries (see note)
½ cup (110g) caster sugar
½ cup (125ml) milk (you can
    use almond or soy milk if
    you prefer)
130g goats cheese
1 tsp lemon juice
Pinch of salt

I designed this recipe a while back for a newsletter, for a couple of friends who made the most delicious goats cheese. It was such a stunner of a recipe that I decided to enter it into the New Zealand Ice Cream awards to really test its quality against actual gelato standards. This little 'instant gelato' recipe won a silver medal no less! If you are trying to imagine what it tastes like, strawberry cheesecake would be the closest thing I can think of. It's a great recipe as it doesn't require churning or a special ice cream machine, or even more than ten minutes of your time!

•

Place all the ingredients in a food processor and process until completely smooth. Serve immediately.

If you aren't going to use it all straightaway, transfer to an airtight container with a lid and keep in the freezer. Take it out of the freezer a good 10 minutes or so before scooping, for a nice soft texture.

•

NOTE: The strawberries need to be hulled and frozen solid.

Baby Strawberry Loaves

MAKES 10 FRIANDS OR
12 MUFFINS

2 eggs
½ cup (110g) sugar
1 cup (280g) plain yoghurt
½ cup (125ml) rice bran oil
1 tsp vanilla extract
1½ cups (225g) plain flour
1½ tsp baking powder
Pinch of salt
1½ cups (about 200g) chopped
    strawberries
Icing or jam to glaze, optional

This is a recipe that evolved from a glut of strawberries in my garden, and uses basic ingredients that I always have on hand. I like to use friand tins for the shape, but you could use muffin tins. The yoghurt instead of butter keeps them tender and moist.

•

Preheat the oven to 190°C fan-forced. Grease 10 friand tins or 12 medium muffin tins.

Whisk the eggs and sugar until smooth then whisk in the yoghurt, oil and vanilla. Sift the flour, baking powder and salt over and gently fold to combine, taking care not to overmix. Fold in the strawberries.

Divide evenly among the tins. Bake for about 30 minutes, until a skewer inserted into the centre of one comes out clean.

Leave to cool in the tins for 10 minutes, then transfer to a wire rack to cool completely.

Spread with icing or glaze with jam, if you like.

•

NOTE: It's best if the eggs and strawberries are at room temperature and the yoghurt isn't chilled – take it out of the fridge a little while before using.

Strawberry Amaretto Slushie

1 cup (220g) caster sugar
⅔ cup (160ml) water
3 cups (about 400g) strawberries,
   hulled and chopped
1 tbsp lemon juice
3 tbsp amaretto (see page 216)
1 cup ice cubes
Mint leaves, to taste (optional)

I'm a huge fan of amaretto. I usually just have it over ice, sometimes as an aperitif, sometimes as a digestif. This is neither – it's a sunny late-afternoon summer indulgence. This recipe is often already half made for me, as I usually have sugar syrup and frozen strawberries on hand.

•

Bring the sugar and water to the boil over high heat, just until the sugar has dissolved. Cool then place into the fridge to chill. Place the chopped strawberries on a tray and freeze until semi frozen.

Place the strawberries into a blender and add the lemon juice, amaretto, ice cubes and mint, if using. Blend until smooth. With the motor running, drizzle the sugar syrup in slowly.

Pour into a shallow tray and freeze until nearly firm. Serve in chilled glasses.

•

NOTE: Resist the temptation to add extra alcohol as the mixture may not freeze. You can always drizzle some over the top when you serve it, if you like.

Strawberry Oat Slice

MAKES 12

3 cups (270g) rolled oats
1½ cups (225g) plain flour
1½ cups (330g) brown sugar
1½ cups (120g) desiccated
  coconut
300g butter, chopped
3 tbsp golden syrup
½ tsp bicarbonate of soda
1½ cups muesli, mixed fruit or
  nuts (see note)
1½ cups (about 200g) frozen
  strawberries (also great with
  frozen rhubarb or blueberries)

This is a variation of a recipe from my mother's café, Eliza's Pantry. The slices were often sold in small bags of half a dozen for 'take away'. Only a few cookies or slices made it to this status – from memory her shortbread was another. This has golden syrup in it, which makes it extra delicious. The technique of heating the golden syrup and butter separately from the other ingredients somehow accentuates the flavour. I was not really a breakfast eater as a kid, but by late morning this was the bomb!

•

Preheat the oven to 180°C fan-forced. Lightly grease a 30cm × 25cm, 3cm deep slice tin and line with baking paper.

Combine the rolled oats, flour, sugar and coconut in a large bowl.

Melt the butter with golden syrup in a large saucepan. Add the bicarb and stir to combine (it will bubble and rise up). Add to the dry ingredients and mix well. Stir in the muesli, fruit or nuts.

Spread the mixture into the prepared tray. Scatter the frozen fruit evenly over the top and press in slightly. Bake for about 40 minutes, until lightly golden.

Cut while warm, but do not remove from the tray until completely cool.

•

NOTE: You can add a mixture of anything you like here, such as choc chips, dried apricots, hazelnuts and sultanas. I often use leftover muesli to prevent waste.

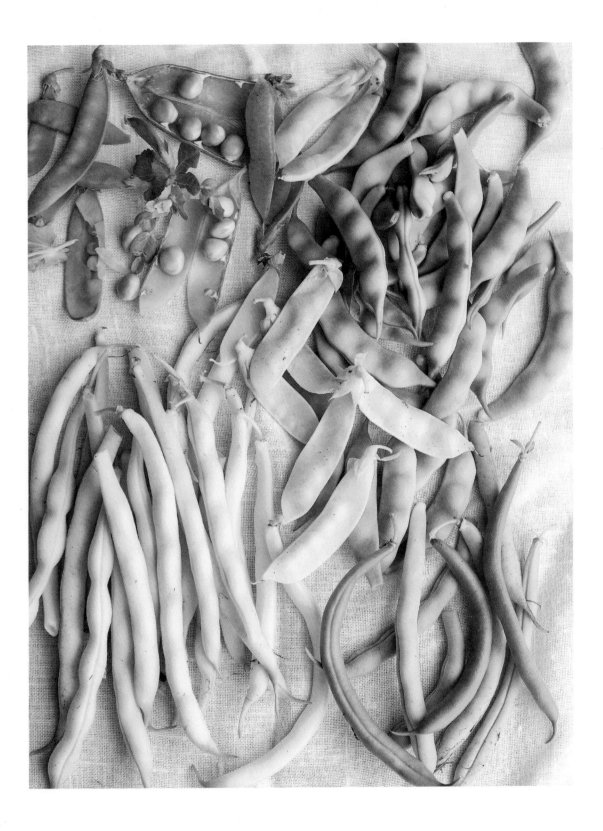

Summer

SOIL

I've heard so many people say that they can't grow anything, but what has really happened is their soil is depleted. Soil is a living organism and the more vibrant it is with microbes and bugs and 'life in general', the better chance you have to grow something. This is a huge topic, and I'm not going to cover it all here. This is simply a nudge to read more, learn more about it – trust me, it will make a HUGE difference. Many of my friends have asked for gardening advice and when I start on the topic of soil, I can see them hesitate, or their eyes glaze over. When they ask what kind of fertiliser they should get for this plant or that plant, I try to explain that you don't need to buy specific fertilisers for specific plants, you want your soil to provide ALL the nutrition for the plant. Like in nature. I've started to compare it to gut health helping the human body. Soil health is the same and there are many ways to improve it, even in small ways.

Gardeners are always talking about compost and worm farms and mulch, with good reason. These are the keys to soil nutrition, bringing life to your soil which in turn will bring life to your plants. You need your soil to have real living microbes, actual life in it rather than synthetic additives. It's a complex structure, that can take several years to develop and improve, but you can start slowly and grow a few things that will help this along. Different plants will contribute different benefits to the soil. Beans are a great example. They are known as a 'nitrogen fixing' plant, often used as a 'cover crop' which means grown specifically for the purpose of replenishing the soil – nature is clever that way. Comfrey is a great pollinator plant, and the leaves are wonderful for soil nutrition.

I have seen aphids in my garden but not lost a plant to them in years, and I think the reasons are twofold. The soil is nutritious, making the plants strong enough to withstand bugs and disease. I have never sprayed any bugs that did appear, so eventually their predators turned up for a free meal and made a home in my garden, helping me out with the aphids ever since.

Before you start a garden I recommend that you check the PH level of your soil, and also know the type of soil that you have. Soil types can vary from sandy to heavy clay and everything in between, but it is not difficult to improve the soil and make it suitable for growing your vegetables. Don't try to take on too much at once, as there is a ton of information out there and it can be overwhelming. I would also recommend taking a few long walks around your neighbourhood to see what grows well in your area.

Ultimately the more effort you put into the health of your soils, the more rewarding your garden will be.

Passionfruit

Passionfruit have the most striking, exotic blooms and remind me of something you would see in a Dr Seuss illustration. Along with their lush shiny green leaves they make a wonderful way to hide an ugly fence or shed. While they are big and take a fair amount of space, the type of space they take is very useful in a compact garden.

They are a tropical plant but given the right aspect in a garden you may be able to entice them along. Just be prepared for quite a lot of leaf drop when it gets cold. They are cold-tolerant enough to be grown outside but they do like warm feet, so mulch them. They handle being in a container or pot as long as they are well fed and have something for their tendrils to creep over and attach to.

I previously cut mine all the way back to the ground, because it had grown in an inconvenient space and I thought I was killing it. But, ironically, it flew back into action the next spring with the most growth and the most fruit I've ever seen! I believe the more orthodox way of handling them is to trim all the fruit tendrils back in autumn after harvesting (about a third of the plant). The new growth will provide the fruit next year. Feel free to use one of the trimmings as a cutting – they are very easily propagated this way.

They really only need watering in the height of summer, so watch the leaves for signs of stress if you are not sure.

Passionfruits do have bug predators – vine hoppers – and they're persistent. I don't spray with pesticides, but if you do, try to get them in the nymph stage when they are fluffy little critters. I have so much bird life around me now (from years of not spraying), that they eat all the bugs. Now I can get rid of an infestation by spraying the plant with water a couple of times a day, especially in the evening. This sends all the bugs flying, which attracts the resident fantails (pīwakawaka),

who happily snack on them. I will have to do this for about a week to get them all. The larger vine hoppers are much easier to squish individually, and don't generally appear in the numbers of the nymphs.

Passionfruit can also be susceptible to some fungal diseases, usually arising from humid conditions, so watering in the morning and removing any manky foliage from around the base of the plant can help.

This is one of the plants where all the fruit can ripen quickly at the same time, so scoop pulp into an ice cube tray to freeze individual portions for later use. Or heat some sugar syrup and add some pulp. If you add a little lemon juice, it will keep quite well in the fridge.

When the fruits fall from the vine, pick them up and set aside for a few days until they start to wrinkle just a little bit. This is how you know they are perfectly ripe and, trust me, it's worth the wait.

My favourite uses for passionfruit are very simple. I'll have it on top of my yoghurt and cereal, or in any cold drink (it's delicious in ginger beer and prosecco alike).

A simple delight, really just a Bellini with passionfruit instead of peach but just as delicious, and such a stunning way to enjoy that very first fruit from the vine. You could use the syrup below instead of fresh passionfruit if you like, but this is definitely a great way to herald the beginning of the passionfruit season! Just put a few spoonfuls of passionfruit into a glass and top up with prosecco.

Syrup

Combine 2 cups water and 2 cups sugar in a saucepan over medium heat and stir to dissolve the sugar. Bring to the boil. Add 1 cup passionfruit pulp and simmer for a few minutes. If you want fewer seeds, then strain it and add back the amount you want. Cool then keep in the fridge for up to 1 month. It will keep longer (up to 2 months) if you add a teaspoon of citric acid or squeeze of lemon juice.

Frozen Yoghurt

Mix about 2 cups of plain yoghurt (Greek or full fat) with ½ cup runny honey (add a little warm water if needed to make it 'runny' but include that in the ½ cup measurement). Add passionfruit pulp to your liking and swirl it through. Freeze in an airtight container, or in ice block moulds.

Combine lemonade, passionfruit pulp, mango juice, a squeeze of lemon juice and several slices of lemon (quantities to your taste). Add crushed mint sprigs and serve chilled over lots of ice. White rum is optional!

Sorbet

Use the passionfruit syrup (across) and add a little lime juice. Churn in an ice cream machine, or freeze in ice block moulds. The sorbet is pretty served in the left-over passionfruit shells.

White chocolate

Melt white chocolate buttons, add scooped out passionfruit and gently swirl through the chocolate. Line a shallow tray with greaseproof paper and spread the chocolate over. Sprinkle with coconut shreds if you want to, then leave it to set (in the fridge if the weather is hot).

Frosting

Simply add pulp or syrup to your favourite frosting, replacing any liquid you would have used.

Passionfruit truffles

Process equal amounts of broken up gingernut (or plain) biscuits, chopped cream cheese and desiccated coconut in a food processor until combined. Stir in passionfruit pulp to taste. Roll into balls and chill. To make these really special, dip in melted white chocolate to coat.

Passionfruit dressing

Combine ½ cup Greek yoghurt, pulp of 6 passionfruits, 1 tbsp honey, 2 tbsp apple cider vinegar and ¼ cup olive oil in a jar with a lid and shake thoroughly. Season with salt and pepper to taste. Keep chilled and use within a day or so. Delicious on any salad.

Passionfruit Yoghurt Cake

SERVES 12

BISCUIT BASE
250g plain biscuits
1 tsp ground ginger
125g butter, melted

YOGHURT FILLING
8 gelatine leaves
50ml Curaçao
500g sweetened vanilla yoghurt
700ml cream, whipped
Passionfruit syrup, to taste
   (see page 76)

This is dreamy, light and melts in your mouth. Tangy passionfruit syrup balances beautifully with the creamy filling, making this dessert seem way more decadent than it is!

Brush a 20cm round springform tin with melted butter and line the base with baking paper.

To make the base, finely crush the biscuits and mix together with the ginger and butter. Press firmly over the base of the tin, going carefully into the edges. Place in the fridge for 10–15 minutes to chill and firm up, while making the filling.

For the filling, place the gelatine leaves into a bowl and cover with cold water. Leave for a couple of minutes to soften. Squeeze out the excess water and add to a small saucepan with the Curaçao. Heat gently over low heat, stirring occasionally, until dissolved. Transfer to a bowl to cool slightly. Stir into the yoghurt then fold in the whipped cream.

Pour over the chilled base and refrigerate overnight, to set.

Serve drizzled with passionfruit syrup.

Artichokes

Artichokes are magnificent to grow even if you don't want to eat them. They are architecturally tall plants with long silver leaves that dwarf everything in early summer. If I had a flower garden, I would be tempted to grow these at the back of the garden purely for the height and colour, and of course the enormous purple flower heads that attract all the bumblebees. These plants are also spectacular in a container.

They can be grown from seed, or you can usually purchase small plants from the herb section of the garden centre. I'm not sure why they are classified like this, they are very nutritious, but not what I would technically classify as a herb. They are probably most closely related to a thistle.

Growing from seed takes a little longer, and may not be entirely true to its parent plant. This can be a fun way to have different varieties of artichokes, but for certainty you will need to gather 'pups' (young plants that grow near the base of the old plant) or divide roots from a known plant.

In warm climates, which is their preference, they grow as a type of perennial, offering up pups along their stem. They can be grown in colder climates as annuals, but if well-mulched in winter they will come up again. The most common cause of them not making it through winter will be their roots getting too soggy and rotting. The main thing to remember when planting is the size they mature to, and allowing enough space for this. They do well in full sun, and with a lot of rainfall they will quickly run to extra growth and flower buds … which is a good thing, as this is the edible part of the plant.

They like a lot of compost or manure and to be fed quite heavily, so top them up each spring with a layer of food and mulch – especially if you are growing them in pots.

For eating they are picked while unopened, with the 'petals' still quite tight. About the size of a large apple is best, as there is less work in preparing them in the kitchen. They usually send up a main bud, which you will have to pick first for the others to continue growing, so it does provide a staggered harvest. If your plan is to preserve them, you may need more than one plant. The side buds will be a little smaller than the original one from the centre of the stem.

When they have finished producing, cut the stem back to a few inches above the ground, or just above any new shoots. Sometimes I leave a flower or two for the bees over summer and the plant will naturally die back and fall over. This seems to encourage new shoots, but a very untidy look for the garden. The seed heads are reminiscent of giant dandelions with fluff attached to each seed to carry it away on a breeze.

The main pest I have found on my artichoke is the earwig, and the damage is mainly superficial. I drop all my artichokes into a bucket of water before I take them into the kitchen, which causes any creatures to come out from the nooks and crannies, so I don't have any escapees running around my kitchen.

RECIPES

Stuffed Artichokes

Juice of 1 lemon
6 artichokes
2–3 tbsp olive oil
5 anchovy fillets (and a little
of their oil)
3 garlic cloves, crushed
1 cup (70g) breadcrumbs
(made from day-old bread)
1 cup fresh herbs (parsley, sage,
thyme, oregano)
¼ cup (50g) capers
⅓ cup (25g) finely grated grana
padano, pecorino or parmesan
150ml white wine

I thoroughly look forward to making these each spring. They have the best crispy, crunchy topping, with all the traditional Italian flavours throughout – somehow reminiscent of the crispy corners of a lasagne. Eating these is the vegetable version of eating spare ribs, where things can get a little messy, but it's worth it!

•

Preheat the oven to 190°C fan-forced. Add the lemon juice to a large bowl of cold water. Trim the artichokes by cutting roughly ⅓ off the tops to make a flat surface. Cut the stalks off, level with the artichoke base. Remove some of the tough outer leaves. Pry open the centre and scoop out any of the inner fluffy choke. Place each prepared artichoke into the lemon water as it is done.

Heat a little of the olive oil (and use some of the oil from the anchovies too) in a frying pan over medium heat and add the anchovies and garlic. As the anchovies start to 'melt', add the breadcrumbs and a little more oil. Stir constantly so they don't stick. As the breadcrumbs turn golden add the herbs and capers, and cook for another minute or two.

Take off the heat, stir in the cheese and season with salt and pepper. Leave to cool.

Use a teaspoon to 'stuff' the mixture in between the leaves and into the centre of the artichokes. Arrange standing upright in a baking dish and drizzle any of the remaining oil over. Bake for 20 minutes, then pour the wine into the baking dish. Bake for a further 20 minutes, until the tops are crispy and the artichokes are cooked through (test with a skewer). Cool slightly before serving.

Fried Artichokes with Caper & Lemon Mayonnaise

Juice of 1 lemon (see note)
4 artichokes
Vegetable oil, to deep-fry

**CAPER AND LEMON
MAYONNAISE**
2 tsp capers in brine, drained
2 tsp olive oil
1 tsp brine from the capers
1 tsp finely grated lemon zest
⅓ cup (100g) mayonnaise

This is typically a peasant dish, kind of like an Italian version of crispy potato skins. If you have a favourite dip then use that, but I've always loved the salty, zesty flavour combination in this mayonnaise. It makes the fried artichokes particularly moreish, and masks the richness of the crispy leaves. A great alternative is the yoghurt sorrel sauce on page 110.

•

To make the mayonnaise, chop half the capers and set aside. Heat the oil in a small frying pan over medium heat. Add the whole capers and stir until crisp. Drain on paper towels to cool slightly then chop. Combine with remaining ingredients, including set-aside capers. Keep in the fridge until serving time.

Add the lemon juice to a large bowl of cold water. Trim the artichokes by cutting roughly ⅓ off the tops to make a flat surface. Trim the stalks to about 5cm long. Remove some of the tough outer leaves. Cut the artichokes in half lengthways if they are smaller or into quarters if they are larger. Scoop out any of the inner fluffy choke. Place each prepared artichoke into the lemon water as it is done.

Drain the artichokes well and pat with paper towel to dry as much as possible. Half fill a large saucepan with oil and heat over medium-high heat.

Deep-fry the artichokes in batches for 3 minutes each batch or until lightly golden. Drain on paper towel. Reheat the oil and fry again in batches for 2–3 minutes, or until golden brown and completely crispy. Drain on paper towel.

Serve with the mayonnaise for dipping.

•

NOTE: Make sure you grate the zest from the lemon for the mayonnaise before you juice it!

Beans

Beans are super easy to grow from seed. They are annuals, so every spring you must start a fresh set of seedlings. The exception is the scarlet runner bean plant, which will grow back each year. They are the most rewarding plant to grow from seed, as they leap to life easily and are lovely robust little seedlings to transplant.

I've always preferred fresh beans, as opposed to buying them frozen, but even in season they are fairly expensive, so growing your own is always a good idea. The other bonus is that the plants themselves are good for the soil, as they are 'nitrogen fixing' plants. At the end of the season cut them to ground level, and compost the tops or just drop onto the garden directly as mulch.

There are two main types: dwarf and climbers. Climbers are going to need staking, or can be grown up a trellis or fence. I always feel that climbers are more productive, but that is purely anecdotal. Make sure to pick every couple of days during the season, as this actively encourages them to produce more.

Like tomatoes, there is a huge range of heirloom varieties, and you can have fun trying out different varieties to find your favourites. I have grown several different ones each year to settle on mine. All have been very easy to grow and don't have too many pest problems, although I find the slugs can reach the dwarf beans, but not the climbers.

When planting out the bean seedlings, I would recommend covering them for a week or two with some netting (or similar), as blackbirds will come along and rip them out to get at the bean seed that is still in the root system. Even when they don't have anything at the base, birds will just ruthlessly leave them laying uprooted in the garden.

They are the simplest plant to seed save from, as they will grow true to their parent plant. Simply leave a couple of bean pods on the plant until the bean pod is brown and dry at the end of summer. The pod should feel almost crunchy and the seeds will rattle inside.

If you are doing this at the beginning of the season, tie a little piece of string or ribbon to the ones you want to save so that you don't accidently pick them, or leave an entire plant for seed. Once fully dry, pick them and open the pods, then let the seeds dry a little further inside before storing for next year.

The simplest preservation method for beans is to blanch and freeze them. Choose unblemished beans and cook them in a saucepan of boiling water for just 2 minutes, then immediately transfer to a bowl of iced water to stop the cooking process. Lay them out to dry on a tea towel. Spread onto a tray and freeze until firm before putting them in a container or freezer bag. This prevents them clumping together, meaning I can just grab a handful at a time as I want them over winter.

Italian Green Beans

SERVES 4–6

500g beans (green beans or butter
    beans, or a combination)
1 tbsp extra virgin olive oil
1 anchovy fillet
1 shallot, finely chopped
1 garlic clove, finely chopped
1 tsp capers, or to taste
Pinch of dried chilli flakes
500g tomatoes, chopped
Chopped parsley, to taste
Shaved parmesan, to serve

This is true southern Italian seasonal eating. These ingredients grow together and are harvested together, and not surprisingly taste great together too.

•

Trim the picked end of the beans. I like to leave them whole, but you can cut them in half if you like.

Bring a large pot of water to boil then add some salt. Cook the beans for 1–2 minutes, until slightly crunchy (you could steam them instead if you prefer). They only need to cook briefly, as they will cook a little more with the tomatoes. Refresh beans in iced water. Drain and lightly shake dry.

Meanwhile, heat the oil in a large frying pan over medium heat. Add the anchovy and cook, stirring, until it starts to 'melt', then add the shallot, garlic, capers and chilli flakes. Cook for about 2 minutes, until the shallot becomes translucent. Add the tomatoes, reduce the heat slightly and simmer gently until the tomatoes are very soft. Stir in the parsley.

Add the beans to the tomato mixture. Simmer for 5–10 minutes, until the beans are tender. Season with salt and pepper to taste.

Serve hot, warm or at room temperature, garnished with parmesan.

Green Bean Panzanella

50ml olive oil
1 onion, finely chopped
20g butter
Handful of sage leaves
4 garlic cloves, finely sliced
800g beans, trimmed to
    preferred size
2 cups (140g) breadcrumbs
    (made from day-old bread)
½ cup (70g) hazelnuts, roasted
    and roughly chopped
Handful of parsley
1 lemon, zest finely grated, juiced

This dish is just literally my favourite summer garden ingredients, turned into a salad. It makes a great side dish for a BBQ. You don't have to make it just from green beans, you can add broccolini, broccoli stems, kale or asparagus spears – it is open to interpretation, but the beans are pretty delicious.

•

Heat the oil in a large frying pan over medium heat. Add the onion and cook until softened and lightly browned. Increase the heat to medium-high and add the butter, sage and garlic. Cook for a couple of minutes then add the beans.

Cook, stirring often to prevent sticking to the base of the pan, until the beans are tender. A few little crispy bits are actually quite nice through the dish so don't worry too much.

Add the breadcrumbs and cook, stirring to ensure they don't stick to the base of the pan, until they start to crisp up. Turn the heat off and stir in the hazelnuts and parsley. Add lemon zest and juice to taste, and season with salt and pepper.

Tomatoes

Tomatoes are one of my favourite vegetables to grow. At first I grew standard varieties, but quickly discovered that it made more sense to grow more interesting heirloom types. If I wanted to buy standard tomatoes, they were at the farmers' market at a reasonable price. For the same amount of effort, I had an array of large, colourful, fat, flavoursome tomatoes.

They are seasonal and love long hot summer days. I've tried once or twice to grow them year-round in my greenhouse, and it wasn't worth the effort. The plants straggled along for ages, producing a couple of small tomatoes in return for months of care.

Tomatoes can be classified as either determinate or indeterminate types. Determinate are smaller bushy plants that don't usually need staking or extra pruning and are great for growing in pots. They will have one main crop that will generally ripen all at once, which is great for preserving, when you want a lot of fruit without needing to have a lot of plants.

Indeterminate plants grow taller and usually require staking and the regular removal of laterals (side shoots). They have a more constant supply of fruit in smaller quantities, just one or two tomatoes ripen at a time so they can potentially provide fresh tomatoes all summer long. This is my favourite type as it suits my style to just pick a few tomatoes every day or so.

Once past these two main genres of tomatoes, the choice is endless in colour, flavour, size, lycopene levels and style.

They are very easy to grow from seed if you are a beginner, and generally cheap if you buy the seedlings in spring. Choose a sunny spot in your garden. They do benefit from a bit of mulch around their base. It is a good idea to set up the supports prior to planting so that you don't damage the root system later on.

As they grow, 'remove the laterals' is the common advice – simply keep one main stem and remove any new stem growth that appears in the 'elbow' of a main leaf and the main stem. These mini tomato plants can be popped in water on your windowsill, where they will grow new roots quite quickly and can be planted out or given away.

Watering over a dry summer is important. They prefer a deeper drink every few days, rather than every day.

Really the only other task is to remove any extra leaves, as they need good air circulation through the plant. Remove any leaves that are damaged or diseased first, then any that are touching the ground, then any touching each other. Don't leave them as mulch just in case any of them were diseased – you don't want to contaminate your plant.

Companion plant your tomato with basil and watch your caprese salad grow!

RECIPES

Tomato Sauce

1.8kg heirloom or homegrown
    tomatoes, chopped
1 large onion, chopped
1 cooking apple, chopped
475ml malt vinegar
450g brown sugar
55g salt
1½ tsp ground white pepper
¼ tsp cayenne pepper
1 tsp allspice
1 tsp ground cloves

This recipe in Nonna's book has 'Mum's' in the top right-hand corner, so this is actually my great-grandmother's recipe, from Napoli. Simply put: we grew up on this. It's one of those sauces that gets better as it ages. A bottle of this is pure gold.

I used to make this with supermarket tomatoes, but decided I needed something fleshier and with less water content. This was before heirloom tomatoes were readily available, so I contacted an Italian guy in Wellington whose family had had the foresight to bring tomato seeds with them on the journey here from Stromboli. He had been growing them, and seed saving, every year since.

Months after we spoke, an envelope turned up in my letterbox. It had my address in tiny cursive writing on the front and nothing inside, or so I thought. On closer inspection I found about a dozen loose seeds in the far corner of the envelope. Since then, the tomatoes I have dubbed 'Stromboli tomatoes' have been grown in my garden every year, with me carefully saving the seeds.

The change in tomatoes has made a difference to the sauce. It's not the end of the world if you use the standard reds. Honestly, the sauce is so good that I would use any tomatoes rather than have no sauce at all!

•

Combine all the ingredients in a large, heavy-based saucepan. Bring to the boil then simmer uncovered over low heat for 3 hours, stirring occasionally.

Use a stick blender to puree until smooth, and then strain through a sieve. Alternatively, use a moulis to puree and strain.

Reheat if necessary, and use a funnel to transfer to sterilised bottles (see page 249) while hot. Seal bottles tightly.

This will last for months in a cool dark place, and is best stored in the fridge once opened.

•

NOTE: Add more cayenne if you would like a spicier version. The heat of the cayenne is very prominent for the first few days, but mellows into the sauce as the flavours combine with time.

Tomatoe Sauce   (Hum's)

8 lbs Ripe Tomatoes
1 Qt. Vinegar
¼ lb. Salt
1 Tablespoon White Pepper
½   "   Cayenne Pepper
¼ Ozs. Allspice
1   "   Ground Cloves
2 Large Onions
8 lb Brown Sugar
2 Nice Cooking Apples.

Method.
Put all in saucepan and boil for
3 hours strain through Colander &
bottle while hot

House Picket

lb 1 plum
lb 2 suger
lb 5 folwer

Peanut Goolash

Pizza or Pasta Sauce

MAKES 4 × 500ML JARS

4 anchovy fillets
Splash of olive oil
1.5kg tomatoes, chopped
Handful of basil leaves (see note)

This is the sauce I make to use throughout the year. I use it as a base for various pasta sauces, or spread directly onto pizzas before I add the toppings. It's really the only 'preserving' I commit to in any quantity. It can be stored in sterilized jars, or frozen if you have the freezer space.

I highly recommend the addition of the anchovies, even if you don't like them. The actual flavour is difficult to detect, adding an umami undertone rather than a fishy taste. For a vegan version, leave out the anchovies, but not the step of returning it to the pan, just use a little olive oil instead.

•

Place the anchovy fillets and a little of their oil into a saucepan, and add a splash of olive oil. Stir over medium-high heat until they have almost all dissolved. Add the tomatoes, reduce the heat to low and simmer uncovered for about 30 minutes, stirring occasionally, until the liquid of the tomatoes has gone and the mixture is thick.

Add a few leaves of basil per tomato and simmer for a few more minutes, then remove from the heat and cool slightly. Blend the sauce until smooth, or blend a portion of it and then stir it back in to the remaining sauce for a more rustic texture. You could always blend it finer when you go to use it later.

Leave to cool if freezing, then divide portions between freezer bags or airtight containers. Alternatively, divide between hot sterilised jars (see page 249), seal tightly and turn upside down to cool.

This will last for months in a cool dark place, and is best stored in the fridge once opened.

•

NOTE: You may prefer a different herb, thyme or oregano are great alternatives. I often change the herb as the season moves on, depending on what's happening in the garden, but definitely add something.

Simple Marinara Sauce

1 tbsp olive oil
1 onion, diced
5 garlic cloves, crushed
1 tbsp dried chilli flakes
1kg tomatoes, cores removed,
    chopped
2 cups soft herbs (such as parsley,
    sage, oregano and thyme),
    chopped

*I like to use this sauce on pasta, and freeze whatever is left for
another meal.*

Heat the oil in a large saucepan. Add the onion, garlic and chilli
and cook over medium heat for 10 minutes, until very soft but
not coloured.

Add the tomatoes and bring to a simmer. Reduce the heat to low
and cook uncovered for about 90 minutes, stirring occasionally,
until very soft and pulpy. Stir in the herbs.

Bottled Spaghetti

1.4kg tomatoes, chopped
1 large onion, chopped
1 tbsp salt
½ cup (110g) white sugar
½ cup (125ml) balsamic vinegar
Pinch of cayenne pepper
250g spaghetti

This is the Italian version of tinned spaghetti, before that even existed! It's a lot tastier too. Simply tip out and heat in a pan on those days when you want a shortcut. It lends itself well to having basil or freshly ground black pepper added when it's being heated to serve. I don't have a big enough pot or enough preserving jars to make this quantity, so my recipe is a smaller batch. But in the old days if you wanted tomatoes in winter, this is what you did. There isn't much of a method on the handwritten version, because it was made so often. It's perfect to take camping or to the holiday house, and works well as a cold pasta dish too. This is best made in the height of tomato season when the tomatoes are literally too juicy for a lot of other recipes, because it has no other liquid added.

•

Combine all the ingredients except the spaghetti in a large, heavy-based pan. Bring to the boil then reduce the heat to low. Simmer uncovered for an hour, stirring occasionally to ensure it doesn't stick, until reduced and thickened.

Cool slightly, then use a stick blender (or food processor) to blend until smooth, or to your desired texture.

Bring a large pot of salted water to the boil. Cook the pasta, as per packet instructions, until slightly al dente. Meanwhile, reheat the sauce.

Drain pasta and add to the sauce. Toss to coat the pasta thoroughly with the sauce. While piping hot, transfer to sterilised jars (see page 249). Place the lid on and work out any air pockets, then fill again.

Seal jars tightly and turn upside down. Leave to cool. Store in a cool dark place for up to 3 months.

•

NOTE: To use, simply empty the contents of a jar into a pan and heat. Add fresh basil or chilli if you like, and top with grated parmesan.

Tomato Caper Sauce with Parmesan Fish

Plain flour, for dusting the fish
4 blue cod fillets
3 eggs
¼ cup (60ml) milk
Chopped fresh herbs (such as
    parsley, thyme or oregano),
    to taste
½ cup (40g) finely grated
    parmesan
Butter or olive oil, for frying

TOMATO CAPER SAUCE
2 tbsp olive oil
1 onion, finely chopped
2 slices pancetta or streaky bacon
4 large tomatoes, chopped
5 garlic cloves, crushed
1 tsp lemon zest
½ tsp paprika
¼ tsp cayenne pepper, optional
2 tbsp tomato paste
1 cup (250ml) water
1 cup (250ml) white wine
1 cup combined oregano and
    parsley leaves, finely chopped
100g butter, chopped
¼ cup (50g) capers

This sauce is essentially a 'cooked salsa' to serve on fish, chicken or even beans, rather than as a pasta or pizza sauce (although go right ahead!). It's a summer flavour bomb and goes with everything. Most memorable for me growing up was this sauce served on blue cod, so that's what I'm giving you here. If you like, make a bigger batch of the sauce and keep it in the fridge or freezer to have on hand for a quick meal.

•

To make the sauce, heat the oil in a large, deep frying pan over medium-high heat. Add the onion and cook until translucent, then add the pancetta and cook until crispy.

Add the tomatoes, garlic and lemon zest. Cook for a few minutes, until the tomatoes have reduced down a little, then add the spices, tomato paste, water, wine and half the herbs. Simmer for about 10 minutes, until it thickens. Add the butter and stir until melted and combined.

Remove from the heat and add the remaining herbs and capers (if you want, you could fry the capers in a little butter until crispy first). Season with salt and pepper to taste and set aside.

Season the flour with salt and pepper then use to lightly dust the fish. I do this by placing a few tablespoons of seasoned flour to a bag, then adding the fillets and shaking gently to coat evenly.

In a shallow bowl, lightly whisk the eggs and milk together, then stir in the herbs and parmesan.

Heat the butter or olive oil in a large frying pan over medium heat. Dip the fillets into the egg mixture and place into the pan (you may need to spoon a little of the herbs and cheese left in the dish on top of them). Cook for about 5 minutes each side, until lightly golden brown and just cooked through.

Reheat the sauce and serve with the fish on top.

•

NOTE: You could swap the blue cod for monk fish, or talk to your fishmonger for other alternatives.

Tomato with Whipped Feta

4 tbsp honey
½ tsp chilli seeds
1 tbsp butter
2 tbsp capers
500g mixed heirloom (or
    homegrown) tomatoes, sliced
    (little ones can be left whole)
½ small red onion, finely chopped
Small handful of Italian parsley,
    roughly chopped

WHIPPED FETA
80g feta
40g sour cream (or yoghurt)
½ garlic clove, minced
1 tbsp lemon juice
1 tsp olive oil
Lemon zest and cracked pepper
    (optional)

We love the height of summer, when heirloom tomatoes are rich and sweet, ripened on the vine, and the subtleties of flavour in the varieties are pronounced. This tomato medley salad plays on those flavours with a contrasting whipped feta and a sweet honey-chilli drizzle. Make extra of the whipped feta and the honey-chilli drizzle to reconstruct this later as a dip with other garden goodies. Though, honestly, it is best with fresh tomatoes – an addictive combination.

•

To make the whipped feta, blend the feta and sour cream in a food processor until smooth, then stir in the remaining ingredients by hand. Chill until required.

In a small pot, heat honey until runny (no need to simmer or boil) then add chilli seeds and stir thoroughly.

Meanwhile, melt butter in a small pan and fry capers until crispy. Leave to cool

Layer whipped feta on the base of the plate, followed by tomatoes, capers, red onion and parsley. Drizzle with the honey chilli just before serving, and season with salt and pepper to taste.

Fried Green Tomatoes

SERVES 6

½ cup (75g) plain flour
¼ cup (60ml) milk
3 eggs
1 cup (170g) cornmeal
   (or fine breadcrumbs)
4 large firm green tomatoes
Butter or olive oil, for frying

YOGHURT SORREL SAUCE
Small handful French sorrel leaves,
   finely chopped
1 garlic clove
1 tbsp olive oil
1 tbsp honey
100g plain yoghurt

This is one way to preserve some of your tomato harvest. I prepare these as per the recipe, but freeze them instead of cooking them. This this recipe is very easy to scale up or down – just do one tomato if you feel like it – but if you are like me and really dislike the whole milk/egg/breadcrumb event, then make the effort worthwhile and do a whole lot in one go!

I grow varieties of green tomatoes (not just unripe red tomatoes). The variety I like is called Aunt Ruby's German Green, which is a brilliant way to defeat the birds, who are waiting for the colour to change as their clue.

This recipe is a recreation of a dish I tried and fell in love with at a farmers' market in Hawai'i. I figured out the recipe when I got home, and it's been on rotation every summer since. They make a great filling for a vegetarian slider.

•

To make the sauce, blend the sorrel and garlic. Add the olive oil, then stir in the honey and yoghurt. Chill in the fridge until ready.

Place the flour into a shallow dish and season with salt and pepper. Whisk the milk and eggs in another shallow dish, and spread the cornmeal into a third shallow dish.

Core the tomatoes and then cut into 1cm thick slices. Dredge each slice in the flour, then egg, then cornmeal.

Heat the butter or olive oil in a frying pan over high heat. Fry tomato a few slices at a time, until lightly golden on both sides. Drain on paper towel.

Serve with yoghurt sorrel sauce for dipping.

Mediterranean Tray Bake

SERVES 10

2 tomatoes

2 capsicums

2 carrots

2 zucchini

1 eggplant

2 stems of rosemary

2 garlic bulbs, cut in half crossways

12 kalamata olives

Large drizzle of olive oil

Baby spinach and/or watercress, toasted pine nuts and lemon juice or verjuice, to serve

This is one of my 'lazy' go-to recipes that has a base line of tomatoes, garlic, olives and olive oil. Everything else is whatever has popped up in the garden as part of the orchestra. I add in chopped up pieces of sausage sometimes, but you'll develop your own riff on this, I promise. It is lovely tossed through couscous, and makes great leftovers for lunch the next day.

•

Preheat the oven to 190°C fan-forced and line 2 large baking trays with baking paper.

Cut all the vegetables into similar sizes so that they cook evenly. Leave the rosemary as full stems so that you can remove them later.

Drizzle vegetables, rosemary, garlic and olives with olive oil and toss until coated. Arrange onto prepared trays and season with salt and pepper. Bake for 25–30 minutes until tender and lightly golden. Remove rosemary stems.

Serve on a bed of baby spinach and/or watercress, sprinkled with toasted pine nuts and drizzled with a squeeze of lemon juice or verjuice (see page 234).

•

NOTE: Leftovers tossed through some couscous with fresh mint for lunch the next day is amazing.

Pumpkins & Zucchinis

Pumpkin has never been a glamour vegetable, but I'm sure its day is not too far away. I adore the sweetness of oven-roasted pumpkin – often roasting them with the intention of making a pie or soup, but eating it all before I get that far.

If you have the space to let these guys trail around your garden then you should. Growing them is a cinch – definitely in the low-maintenance, beginner category – and they grow so big and lush that it's a really rewarding experience. A fun thing to do with the kids is to grab a packet of seeds and see who can grow the biggest pumpkin. It's a similar thing with zucchini – it's so tempting to fill your garden with them in early spring, because they grow big and lush so quickly.

They need the whole of summer to do their thing, so plant the seeds (absolutely grow them from seed) in spring after the last frosts, or at least keep seedlings indoors until after the last frost.

Both like a sunny position and lots of compost or organic matter to get them going. Often these guys will germinate in your compost or worm farm from discarded seeds in your veggie scraps. I find this amazing as I spend a lot of time creating the perfect seed-raising mix, but nature just does its own thing.

As they grow out in long runners, you will need a bit of space for them, or grow them up a frame. There is definitely a trade off to growing these, as they do take up a lot of space, and in season aren't that expensive to buy. When I had a smaller garden, I didn't grow them as I was willing to compromise to save my space for other veggies. They are far lower down in the 'dirty dozen' list of commercial crops that get sprayed, so I figured buying them wasn't so bad. I now have a bigger garden and very little self-control – so plenty of pumpkins and zucchini.

Pumpkin, zucchini, melons and squash are all related, so male and female flowers will appear on the one vine, but will also cross pollinate with the others. The benefit of this is lots and lots of well pollinated fruit. The drawback is that there is no guarantee that seeds collected will be exactly like their parent plant.

As the fruit sets on the longer trailing vines, just nip off the end of the main tendril so that it puts its growth into the pumpkin, rather than producing more leaves and runners. Over a really hot summer you will need to water them a little at the base of the plant in the morning or evening, especially if you have seen the leaves sag during the day. It really helps with the size of the fruit later on.

If you have a shorter summer growing season, choose a smaller variety of pumpkin, so that it has time to ripen over the season. I tend to grow butternuts (because they are my personal favourite) and one other variety every year – usually one I haven't tried before, just in case there is something out there more delicious than a butternut.

As the fruits develop, especially the pumpkin and melon, slot a piece of wood or dry straw under them, so the moisture of the ground doesn't affect them. They are usually harvested once the plant has died back. When you cut the pumpkins from the vine, leave at least 5cm (more if you can) of stem attached. Let them cure by sitting them in a dry sunny place for a week or two. This toughens the skin, which protects the flesh and allows you to store them for longer. Use any damaged fruits first.

If you are saving seeds, they just need to be cleaned of any flesh residue, dried, then stored in a cool dry place.

Pumpkin Seeds

If you want to eat the pumpkin seeds, which are very nutritious, then the process is a little longer than saving them, but not arduous. They need to be cleaned and dried, then boiled for 2 minutes in lightly salted water. Strain and dry on paper towel. Toss them in olive oil (or any oil), add a little salt and any spices if you like. Roast on a baking tray in a 180°C oven for 10 minutes. You can go sweet or savoury. Try sweet cinnamon – or full blown spicy Mexican. Alternatively leave them plain to add to your homemade muesli or bread.

RECIPES

Zucchini Arancini

SERVES 6

3 zucchini, grated
1 tbsp olive oil
1 onion, finely chopped
2 garlic cloves, crushed
Small handful of parsley,
    finely chopped
Thyme leaves, to taste
1 tsp cracked black pepper
2 eggs
½ cup (40g) finely grated pecorino
½ cup (100g) fine dry
    breadcrumbs, plus more, to coat
100g mozzarella, cut into
    1cm cubes
Vegetable oil, to deep-fry

Arancini are usually made with rice, often from leftover risotto. They have a delectable filling, such as cheese, truffle or ragu and are rolled in breadcrumbs and deep-fried. A lot of Italian cooking represents this style of using up everything, and is the spirit of this dish. If you, like me, are seduced into planting lots of zucchini, unsurprisingly you will have lots of zucchini to use up, so this is for you.

Arancini are Sicilian and southern Italian, and a similar recipe in Rome is called suppli. There are many variations and other names as you travel through Italy, but I think this one, made purely from grated zucchini, is a uniquely New Zealand garden version.

•

Place the grated zucchini into a clean tea towel and wring out over the sink, to remove excess liquid. Place zucchini into a large bowl.

Heat the olive oil in a frying pan over medium-low heat. Gently cook the onion and garlic until translucent, then add to the zucchini.

Add the parsley, thyme, pepper, eggs, pecorino and breadcrumbs. Mix well and season with salt and pepper. If the mixture seems too wet add some more breadcrumbs, though it should be fairly moist.

Take a small handful of the mixture and flatten a little in the palm of your hand. Place a cube of mozzarella in the centre, then enclose with the zucchini mixture and shape into a ball. Roll in the fine breadcrumbs to thoroughly coat.

Half fill a large saucepan with vegetable oil and heat over medium-high heat. Deep-fry arancini in batches until golden brown. Drain on paper towel.

•

NOTE: You can make these in big batches and freeze them after crumbing. They make a great lunch snack in the middle of winter.

Stuffed Zucchini Blossoms

MAKES 6

6 fresh zucchini blossoms with long stems (pick early in the morning for best results)

2–3 tbsp ricotta (see page 230)

Chopped basil, to taste

Finely grated lemon zest, to taste

3 anchovy fillets, halved

1 cup (180g) rice flour

¾ cup (185ml) sparkling water, chilled

Vegetable oil, to deep fry

These are something I look forward to making every year. They are commonplace in Italian restaurants and households, less so here, although they do occasionally grace a few local menus. They are really not that difficult if you have access to the blossoms. I tend to overplant zucchinis purely for the luxury of this dish, and when I'm overloaded with zucchinis later in the season, I'll pick the baby zucchini with the flower still attached, rather than just the male flowers on the stem.

If you only have one plant in the garden you will only get one or two flowers at a time, so I have come across a solution. As the flowers blossom, I pick them and stuff them, then place them in a sealed container in the freezer until I have enough stuffed blossoms to serve. I then bring them out, coat in the batter and deep-fry (no need to thaw). It's literally a two-minute job to stuff and freeze them, and you can vary filling as you go, based on what you have available.

•

Gently tease open the flower and remove the stamen (it's a little bitter to eat). Gently stir the ricotta so that it softens a little, then mix in the basil and lemon zest. Season with salt and pepper.

Spoon mixture into the flowers and lay an anchovy half on top. Don't overfill the blossom, depending on the size it may need just one teaspoon, or a little more. Leave enough room to fully close the petals, with a little twist as they would naturally close. Set aside in the fridge as you fill each blossom, or freeze to use at a later date.

Whisk the rice flour and sparkling water together until smooth.

Half fill a large saucepan with oil and heat over medium-high heat. Drop a little batter in the oil to test – it will 'fizz' and rise to the top when it is hot enough.

Holding a blossom by the stalk, gently dip into the batter to coat evenly. Gently place into the hot oil. Add a couple more, depending on the size of your pan. Cook, turning gently, until the batter is a light golden brown. Drain on paper towel and serve immediately.

Scarpaccia

SERVES 12

500g zucchini, thinly sliced
6 eggs
¾ cup (185ml) milk
1 cup (150g) plain flour
2 tsp sugar
1 cup (80g) finely grated parmesan,
    plus extra, for topping
1 fennel bulb, thinly sliced and
    soaked in cold water for a
    few minutes, then drained
5 garlic cloves, thinly sliced
Zucchini flowers (optional)
Olive oil, to drizzle
Chopped chilli, optional
Fresh thyme, basil or parsley leaves
2 tsp fried capers

This is the quintessential spring dish in Italy – usually only made while the zucchinis are in flower. Scarpaccia means 'old shoe' and there are various stories about how this recipe became named. One version is because an old hand-me-down shoe has been worn by everyone, and this is a recipe that has been handed down. In light of that tradition, don't be afraid to add your own seasonal garden flavours, such as sundried tomatoes or other herbs. This is delicious the next day between two thick slices of white bread and a little of your favourite sauce.

•

Preheat the oven to 180°C fan-forced. Grease a large baking dish (about 35cm × 25cm) or line with baking paper. Lay the zucchini slices out onto a tea towel to dry a little.

Whisk the eggs and milk together in a large bowl, then stir in the flour, sugar and parmesan until you have a smooth batter.

Randomly lay the zucchini, fennel and garlic into the dish, and top with the zucchini flowers (unless you have plenty, in which case layer them through as well). Pour the batter over evenly.

Drizzle with a little olive oil, or sprinkle extra cheese and chilli on top if you like. Sprinkle the herbs and capers over.

Bake for 25 minutes until set and lightly golden on top. Serve at room temperature.

Roasted Butternut Pumpkin Salad

SERVES 4

1 tsp fennel seeds
1 tsp coriander seeds
500g butternut pumpkin, cut into
  1cm thick slices, skin on
2 tbsp olive oil, plus extra for
  topping
½ tsp smoked paprika
20g pine nuts, lightly toasted
⅓ small fennel bulb, thinly sliced,
  tops reserved
6 medjool dates, pitted and sliced
1 shallot, finely sliced
Rind of ½ preserved lemon, finely
  sliced
Handful of herbs such as mint,
  coriander and oregano,
  coarsely chopped
Juice of 1 lemon
200g plain yoghurt

My favourite thing about pumpkins is how sweet they become when they're roasted. I often roast extra with dinner just to be sure that I have enough for a salad the next day, so technically this recipe has come about from leftovers, but by design.

•

Preheat the oven to 200°C fan-forced and lightly oil a large baking tray.

Stir the fennel and coriander seeds in a dry frying pan over medium heat for 1–2 minutes, until fragrant. Cool then lightly crush.

Arrange the pumpkin on the tray. Drizzle with oil and scatter with the crushed seeds and paprika. Season to taste. Cook for 30–40 minutes until tender, golden and the skin has softened, turning once.

Combine the pine nuts, fennel, date, shallot, lemon rind and herbs in a bowl and dress with the lemon juice and a little extra oil. Spread the yoghurt onto a serving platter and top with the pumpkin. Scatter the topping mixture over the pumpkin and top with fennel fronds.

Butternut Cappellacci

500g butternut pumpkin, halved,
    seeds discarded
2 tsp olive oil
80g finely grated parmesan
2 tbsp fine breadcumbs
Pinch of ground nutmeg
Pasta dough (see page 239)

**BROWNED BUTTER &
SAGE SAUCE**
80g butter
Handful of sage leaves (about 20,
    or more)
½ tsp lemon juice

Cappellacci is similar to tortellini, though a little easier. Instead of cutting the pasta sheet into little 'rounds' before you fill them, you make little squares of pasta. The little triangle 'caps' left on the pasta help me to remember its name.

This is a great recipe to make extra of. Freeze the uncooked cappellacci on a tray, then transfer to a bag once frozen. This stops them clumping together. They'll take about 6 minutes to cook from frozen. I love the browned butter and sage combination with pumpkin and it is seasonally ideal, because the pumpkin and sage are ready in the garden at the same time.

•

Preheat the oven to 200°C fan-forced. Brush the cut side of the pumpkin with oil and season with salt and pepper. Place in a roasting pan cut-side down and cook for about 40 minutes, until the pumpkin is tender and the skin is soft. Set aside to cool, then remove the skin. Mash the pumpkin in a bowl with the parmesan, breadcrumbs and nutmeg. Season to taste.

Roll the dough as directed on page 239, finishing at the second last setting. Cut the dough into 7cm squares.

Place a little pumpkin filling into the centre of each square. Moisten the edges with water then fold over to form a triangle. Press the dough together around the filling and try to avoid any trapped air bubbles. Bring the two furthest corner points together and press together to create a little ring. Place on a floured tray until you are ready.

Bring a large saucepan of salted water to the boil. Cook in batches for 2–3 minutes, until al dente.

While they are cooking, to make the sauce, heat the butter in a large pan, until melted and starting to brown slightly. Add the sage leaves and cook until crisp. Stir in the lemon juice.

Add the cooked cappellacci and gently toss together. Serve immediately.

Cucumbers

Cucumbers are so cheap to buy when they are in season that I was slow to start growing them. It wasn't until I noticed local gardeners were leaving them on their gate post or letterbox for others to take home, that I decided to plant them myself, thinking they must be easy to grow! Weird reasoning when I could have just got some from the neighbours, but hear me out. Every book and seed packet will give you an outline of how to grow something, but the best source of information about what will do well in your garden is what is growing well in your neighbourhood. It will also give you a good idea of timing: when to plant and when to expect a harvest.

So now every year I grow a few plants, usually different varieties because it can get tedious having lots of the same type. I plant them in different spots around the garden, so if powdery mildew hits one I am less likely to lose them all. This year the ones that I co-planted in my asparagus patch (permaculture method) were the winners by far. They happily latched on to the stems of asparagus I had let go to seed, sprawled their way through the patch and hid their cucumbers in the straw below. Most importantly they seemed to miss the powdery mildew that took out my entire zucchini crop. If I were the type of person to keep a diary, this is the sort of thing I would note!

Cucumbers like consistent watering, especially once they have set fruit. They can get big quite quickly, so don't be afraid to take a few smaller ones to enjoy as a snack or lunch box item. Remember, the more you pick, the more cucumbers your plant will provide.

I generally raise my cucumbers from seed, planting two seeds together. If they both germinate, I plant them out like that, well mulched, and initially train them to go in different directions. Then I have just the one spot to water on the really hot days.

Because cucumbers are essentially vines, if you have a smaller space, you can train them up a trellis.

The water content of cucumber is too high to freeze them, so developing a good bread and butter pickle or quick pickle-type recipe is important. But in the height of summer their crunchy, crisp water content is a blessing – especially when served chilled with a little soy and sesame.

RECIPES

Cucumber Pickle

MAKES 2 × 500ML JARS

1 tsp dried dill (or 2 tsp chopped
  fresh dill)
2 garlic cloves, finely sliced
2 tsp red chilli flakes
½ red onion, finely sliced
1–2 cucumbers, finely sliced
1½ cups (375ml) water
¾ cup (185ml) apple cider vinegar
1 tbsp sugar
1 tbsp sea salt
½ tsp cracked black pepper

Cucumbers have always been a bit of a 'feast or famine' veggie to grow in my garden – either the plants limp along or overrun my garden. I either pickle the excess or leave them by the letterbox for neighbours to find.

•

Divide the dill, garlic, chilli and onion between sterilised jars (see page 249). Pack in the sliced cucumber.

Place the water, vinegar, sugar, salt and pepper into a saucepan and heat until it boils. Pour the hot liquid over the cucumbers. Seal tightly with the lids. Stand jars upside down onto a cloth to cool, then place into the fridge for up to 1 month.

Dill Gherkins

MAKES 6 × 500ML JARS

2 kg gherkins (or cucumbers,
  cut into batons)
2 tbsp mustard seeds
2–4 bay leaves
Dill sprigs and crowns
800g sugar
700ml white vinegar
40g salt

This recipe is from a lovely Swedish lady called Sylvia, who kindly shared it with me. I need to grow quite a few gherkins to have any chance of having enough ready at one time to pickle, so cucumbers are fine to use here. Cut them into chunky batons to fit the height of the jar, for aesthetics, or cut into slices for ease of popping into a burger down the track.

•

Place the gherkins in a non-metallic bowl with the mustard seeds, bay leaves and dill.

Combine the sugar, vinegar and salt in a saucepan and stir over medium heat until sugar has dissolved. Bring just to the boil, then pour the hot liquid to cover the gherkins. Cover and stand for 24 hours.

Strain the liquid and bring to the boil one more time. Pour over the gherkins, cover and stand for another 24 hours.

Transfer to sterilised jars (see page 249) and seal tightly with lids.

These will keep for up to a year stored in a cool, dark pantry. Once opened, keep in the fridge for up to 1 month.

Chilli Summer Cucumber

2 tsp rice vinegar
2 tsp soy sauce
2 garlic cloves, very finely chopped
2 tsp chilli oil (or to taste)
1 tsp honey
1 tsp sesame seeds, lightly toasted
1 cucumber, sliced

This recipe is not at all from my Italian heritage, but came about simply from a habit of dipping pieces of cucumber into soy sauce! It is super tasty, moreish and refreshing. Something about the combination of cold, sweet, salty and spicy just works.

Stir all the ingredients except the cucumber together in a bowl until evenly combined. Add the cucumber and toss to coat. Leave for a few minutes for the flavours to mingle. Serve cold.

OTHER CUCUMBER IDEAS

If you have grown cucumbers with thicker skin, use a potato peeler to remove alternating stripes of skin. That leaves some nutrients, but less toughness.

For lunchboxes, just cut a length of cucumber – say 5 or 10cm long, then cut into 6 pieces lengthwise. Replace them back together to look uncut and use a rubber band to hold them together. This keeps the inside fresh and is perfect with a small container of hummus or peanut butter for dipping.

Cucumber cups are another favourite little summer snack. Cut the cucumber into 2–3cm slices and scoop out some of the seeds in the middle, without breaking through the base. Fill the little cups with any choice of delicacy, such as a simple diced tomato and olive mixture, or as fancy as crab meat mixed with coconut cream.

Cucumber, avocado, feta and dill make a delicious salad combination, with a squeeze of lemon juice and a sprinkle of finely grated zest. Salty, crispy, creamy – it has it all!

Rhubarb

All the kids who grew up with a rhubarb plant in the garden will know the face-puckering delight of a freshly pulled rhubarb stem dipped in sugar. Nature's own sour patch lolly!

This is a 'must have' for the beginner gardener, as it thrives on neglect and will produce amazing stems for many, many years. It ticks a few boxes for me, because rhubarb is always several dollars a bundle to buy, if you can find it, and is such a healthy vibrant addition to the garden and your breakfast routine.

I used to think it was only seasonal, but there are now varieties that produce year-round. They vary in colour and stem thickness, so I like to have a few different varieties. I always have a thick and green-stemmed seasonal plant, and a slimmer, bright-red 'year-round' one. I have never found the perfect combination of thick stems with bright red all the way up. The garden centres seem to favour the red ones, but if you have minimal garden space the one with fat green stems is the best producer. The slim red ones, however, are very pretty to cook with.

Choose a spot in full sun, or at least lots of good afternoon sun, and also choose somewhere that you don't mind it residing for a number of years. It is aesthetic enough to pop in the corner of a flower garden.

It can be grown from seed, or you could use seedlings from a garden centre to get a little bit of a head start. But the absolute best, if possible, is to find a friend who has an older plant and is dividing the root (more on this later) as this will give you an adult plant producing lots of stalks right from the start.

Preparation is key, but not arduous, for rhubarb. Prepare the soil by digging a deep hole and loading with well-aged manure, compost or sheep pellets. Backfill a little soil, so the plant is not in direct contact with the manure, and cover with soil and a layer of mulch.

In cooler areas these plants will require a little more protection while dormant over winter. A good layer of straw, mulch or even just a thick layer of autumn leaves will do the trick.

When harvesting, twist and pull the outermost stems, rather than cutting them. They should break off neatly. Discard the leaf, as they are poisonous to eat. You can compost them or leave to mulch around the plant, to help reduce weeds.

After a few years you will notice the stalks getting a little overwhelmed for space. Just dig up the entire plant and split it (in half or quarters depending on its size) by quite simply lopping your spade through the middle of it. Replant exactly as you would a new plant, with a big top up of new compost and fertiliser as described above.

I love to turn up to a friend's house with an armload of bright red stems with the giant Dumbo elephant ear leaves still attached. Add your favourite recipe tied in the string or bow and it's a wonderful gift. If you really do have too much, freeze portions of the stewed rhubarb (see page 134), to warm and eat with porridge in winter. You can also just dice it up raw and freeze it as it is, to grab a handful of at a time to cook – almost exactly the way you would with frozen blueberries.

RECIPES

Rhubarb & Custard Pots

STEWED RHUBARB
8 rhubarb stalks, diced
2 tbsp sugar

CUSTARD
½ cup (110g) caster sugar
4 egg yolks
3 tbsp cornflour
½ tsp salt
3 cups (750ml) milk
1 tbsp butter

This is my favourite method for making stewed rhubarb. I love to add some to porridge or have with mascarpone (see page 232) for breakfast. These pots are one of my favourite things to make for bake sales and fundraisers. I keep little jars throughout the year, clean them, remove the labels and store until needed. Then I sterilise them to use. If it's going to be a really hot day, I may make the custard using custard powder instead, just to be safe. If I am making these to have at home, I make the custard using fresh eggs from my chickens.

•

To make the stewed rhubarb, place the rhubarb and sugar into a saucepan and add enough water to just cover. Cook gently over low heat until the sugar dissolves and the rhubarb softens. The moment the rhubarb is cooked, strain the solids from the liquid, keeping both.

Return the liquid to the pan and cook over medium heat until reduced to a slightly thick syrup. Take it off the heat and stir the cooked rhubarb back into the syrup. Leave to cool.

For the custard, whisk the sugar, egg yolks, cornflour and salt in a bowl until pale and creamy. Heat the milk in a saucepan until it just comes to the boil. Slowly add it to the egg yolk mixture, whisking as you go.

Once fully combined, return the mixture to the saucepan and stir over low heat until the custard thickens. Stir in the butter until combined. Transfer to a bowl and leave to cool completely.

Spoon two thirds of the stewed rhubarb into jars (to sterilise, see page 249) then layer with custard and the remaining rhubarb. Serve immediately, or cover and refrigerate for up to 4 days.

•

NOTE: I like to serve sprinkled with a little muesli or hazelnuts.

Rhubarb & Ricotta Breakfast Muffins

MAKES 12

2 cups (300g) plain flour
1½ tsp baking powder
Pinch of salt
2 eggs
1 cup (220g) sugar
1 cup (280g) plain yoghurt
¾ cup (185ml) rice bran oil
    (or light vegetable oil)
½ tsp vanilla essence
3 cups (330g) diced rhubarb
    (about 1cm pieces)
180g ricotta (see page 230)
¾ cup (120g) icing sugar
2 tsp milk

CRUMBLE TOPPING
⅔ cup (100g) plain flour
⅓ cup (75g) brown sugar
½ tsp ground cinnamon
Pinch of salt
60g butter, melted

This recipe has several variations in our house. The rhubarb can easily be swapped for berries or stone fruit (peaches are particularly delicious) and, although ricotta is my favourite, you could substitute cream cheese or custard (see page 134). I always have a surplus of rhubarb in the garden, so I cut it up for this recipe then freeze in individual bags. Come winter, when my rhubarb is not so rampant, I can just grab it from the freezer and throw it into the muffin mixture without even waiting for it to thaw.

•

Preheat the oven to 180°C fan-forced. Grease 12 medium muffin tins, or line with paper liners.

To make the topping, combine the flour, sugar, cinnamon and salt in a bowl, then mix in the butter to a coarse crumb consistency. Set aside.

Stir the flour, baking powder and salt in a large bowl. In a second bowl, whisk the eggs and sugar, then stir in the yoghurt, oil and vanilla. Fold the wet ingredients into the dry ingredients until just combined, then gently fold in the rhubarb.

Drop a tablespoon of the mixture into each tin, then divide ricotta between them, spooning 1 tbsp into the centre of each. Cover with remaining mixture.

Sprinkle the topping over the muffins. Bake for 20–25 minutes, until golden brown and springy to a gentle touch. Cool in the tin for 10 minutes, then transfer them to a wire rack to cool completely.

Stir the icing sugar and milk together until smooth and drizzle over the cooled muffins.

Rhubarb & Custard Torte

6 eggs
¾ cup (165g) caster sugar, plus
extra, for sprinkling
1½ cups (375ml) cream
1½ cups (375ml) milk
6 stale croissants, cut in half
lengthways
6 cups (660g) chopped rhubarb
(about 12 stalks)
30g butter, melted
½ cup (40g) flaked almonds
Icing sugar, to dust, optional

This recipe came about from an overwhelming season of rhubarb. It uses fresh or frozen rhubarb and started as a version of bread and butter pudding, making use of what was loitering in my kitchen, but has since become a star recipe.

•

Preheat the oven to 180°C fan-forced. Remove the base from a 23cm springform tin and lay a large sheet of baking paper over it. Replace the sides, with the excess baking paper hanging out the join. Line the sides with baking paper. Stand on a rimmed baking tray.

Whisk the eggs and sugar until combined, then whisk in the cream and milk. Arrange half the croissants in a layer over the base of the tin, filling any gaps with torn pieces of croissant.

Spread half the rhubarb in a layer over the croissants, then pour one third of the egg mixture over.

Repeat the layers, adding any remaining torn pieces of croissant to the top. Pour all the remaining egg mixture over evenly.

Brush the butter onto any protruding croissant pieces. Sprinkle the almonds and a little extra sugar on top. Stand for about 30 minutes for the croissants to absorb the egg mixture.

Bake for 45 minutes, until set and lightly golden. Leave to cool, so the custard can firm up before removing from the tin. Dust with icing sugar, if using.

Figs

Fig trees are arguably the quintessential Mediterranean fruit tree (though olive and lemon trees might be included in this category). They prefer a warm climate, but if you love figs enough you can make it work. I've heard of Italian families in Chicago literally burying the trees in winter by tipping them sideways into a tree-sized grave and covering them with coffee sacks and logs to protect them from the freezing temperatures and snow. Then they have a grand resurrection every spring. That is incredible dedication, but completely understandable if you love fresh, sun-warmed figs in summer. A hobby of mine is to try and collect heirloom varieties that have family connections. The latest in my garden is a variety given to me by some friends in Nelson, from a fig tree that travelled from Stromboli to D'Urville Island with Angelina Moleta (née Criscillo) in the very early 1900s. Not a lot grows on Stromboli as there is no water source, so there are only a few resilient species to gather.

Figs are ideal candidates for your garden, because they are rarely seen at markets as they don't travel well.

They are fast growing and quick to fruit, so you will be rewarded almost immediately, even if it is just one or two on a tiny twig the first year. After that, almost every stem will have several fruits.

They are tough plants, and fairly pest-free until the figs are ripe – then it is a race against the birds! Fig trees like warm summers and can tolerate a few frosts over winter. The soil should be free-draining, but they are not too particular about the quality of the soil. I do find that my fig tree has handled dry periods a lot better with a thick mulch of leaf litter. While they love the heat, if they get too dry they will abandon their fruit.

Figs are self-fertilising, so you only need the one tree. If you, like me, would like more trees, choose varieties that complement each other seasonally. This extends your fig season, as well as mitigating any weather events that may cause one of the crops to be below average. If you do have hot, dry summers, don't plant out your first tree until late winter or early spring, just to give the roots some time to establish before the summer hits. It's even better to have them as a pot plant for a year or two on your deck (or garden edge) where watering is easy as they adjust to your microclimate, and you can move them inside if the winters are freezing in your area.

Pruning is important and also easy. Start with the branches that are getting in each other's way or rubbing together, anything diseased, and all the suckers that appear (these are perfect for giving away to friends to start their own clone of your tree). Aim to remove about a third of the foliage.

Once the fruit appears, don't be tempted to pick them too soon as they don't ripen well off the tree. They ripen one at a time per branch, so you do get an ongoing supply. You'll know they are ripe when they start to feel soft and change colour, depending a little on the variety. They will also be easy to pick. They only last a few days, but if you end up with too many, they freeze well whole. They are great roasted or in smoothies from frozen.

The leaves are also used in syrups and teas, and most often as a food wrap. I recommend using the younger leaves as they get tough as they get bigger.

RECIPES

USING FRESH FIGS

When figs are in season it's really hard to go past just eating them warm off the tree. In all honesty, fresh figs are best enjoyed as fresh figs, with very little done to them. I haven't found a way to preserve them in a way that truly represents them as well as the magic of eating them fresh. That said, they do have some 'perfect partners' so here are a few of my favourite ways to serve figs …

Caramelised

Sprinkle a little honey, brown sugar or maple syrup on the bottom of a frying pan and heat over medium-high heat. Cut the stem off the figs then cut in half lengthwise. When the pan is hot, place the figs cut side down in the pan. Cook for a couple of minutes, until lightly coloured underneath. Serve with muesli and unsweetened yoghurt, drizzled with some of the honey from the pan.

Gorgonzola-stuffed

This is perfect for a cheese platter. Cut the stems off (quite low) and score a deep cross about two thirds of the way down some figs. Open out the cuts a little and stuff with a teaspoon of gorgonzola, then drizzle with a little honey.

With sliced pears & shaved pecorino

Halve, core and finely slice a pear. Cut the stems from a couple of figs, then finely slice. Arrange alternately on a plate and top with shaved pecorino (or salted ricotta if you have it).

With ricotta, honey & salted pistachios

Cut the stems off figs (cut quite low so you have a flat surface area on top) and score a deep cross into the top. Open out the cuts a little and stuff with fresh ricotta (see page 230). Sprinkle chopped salted pistachios and then drizzle with honey.

Fig & goats cheese tartines

Toast a slice of your favourite sourdough bread. Spread with a layer of goats cheese, then splay a sliced fig on top. Sprinkle with thyme leaves and drizzle with honey.

Amaretto-roasted

To roast the figs, remove the stems, cut in half and lay cut side up in a baking dish. Drizzle with a little amaretto (see page 216) and roast, or cook under the grill, to your liking. While warm, place on top of ice cream (with some of the pan juices) and sprinkle with chopped hazelnuts.

Wrapped in serrano ham

Remove the stems from figs and cut into quarters. Wrap each quarter with a very thin slice of serrano ham. Serve fresh or baked, with a drizzle of honey if you like.

Fresh Fig Salad

SERVES 4

6 fresh figs, stems removed
1 small punnet blackberries
1 pear, cored and thinly sliced
Handful of carrot tops
Handful of rocket
30g toasted hazelnuts, roughly
    chopped
30g hemp hearts

WARM CHILLI HONEY
2 tbsp honey
Finely chopped chilli, to taste

This is a 'snapshot in time' kind of salad from my garden, using elements that are all ready together on the cusp of Autumn.

◆

To make the chilli honey, combine the honey and chilli in a small saucepan. Bring to the boil and then set aside to cool slightly. You do want to serve this warm, so either do it right before serving the salad, or gently reheat just before serving.

Arrange the fruits and leaves on a platter and sprinkle with the hazelnuts and hemp hearts. Serve with the warm chilli honey on the side to drizzle over.

◆

NOTE: If you can't find hemp hearts (try the supermarket or health food stores), you can substitute with a light sprinkle of prepared couscous.

Fig Tarte Tatin

SERVES 4

1 tbsp butter, plus extra, melted,
    to brush
2 tbsp honey
6 sprigs fresh thyme
5 figs, halved
½ onion, cut into thin wedges
1 sheet ready-rolled frozen puff
    pastry, just thawed
40g pecans

This is a rather delicious sweet-but-actually-savoury tart. Once the onion has roasted and morphed into sweet morsels, it's a little hard to tell where this sits. You could almost serve this with ice cream as easily as you would with a crumble of blue cheese or a drizzle of balsamic. Definitely brunch from the garden.

•

Preheat the oven to 180°C fan-forced. In a 22cm (top measurement) heavy based frying pan (preferably cast iron), lightly brown the butter then add half the honey and leaves from 3 sprigs of the thyme.

Place the figs cut side down over the base of the hot pan. Add the onions into the gaps. Cook over high heat for a few minutes, to colour the figs. Remove from the heat.

Lay the pastry over the figs and tuck the edges into the sides of the pan. Brush pastry with melted butter.

Bake for 15–20 minutes, or until the pastry is golden brown. Remove from the oven and place a plate over the top of the pan. Carefully invert the pan so the tart lands on the plate fig-side up.

Heat the remaining honey in the pan and add the pecans, stir to coat. Sprinkle on top of the tart, and garnish with the remaining fresh thyme leaves.

Preserved Baby Figs

500g hard green (unripe) figs
2 cups (440g) sugar
2 cups (500ml) water
1 cinnamon stick
3 wide strips lemon zest
   (without white pith)
½ cup (125ml) amaretto
   (see page 216)

My fig tree in the garden doesn't always do well, but it's glorious when it does. A lot of gardeners will talk about how everything 'should work' if all the correct steps are followed, but sometimes the seasons and the weather have other ideas. If my early fruiting tree gets too hot and dry the tree will just dump all the baby figs, which is devastating. This is an old Italian 'rescue recipe' in a bid to salvage something from the situation (yes, I have a compost and that would have been fine too, but this helps with the pain of the loss). I have since learnt that mulching really well helps regulate the tree a little better, but I have also planted a second fig tree that fruits at a different time of year to help mitigate the weather conditions. I now make this recipe each year regardless. It's a little like a fig version of a glace cherry.

Rinse the figs and fully remove all the stems. Poke a large hole from top to bottom with a clean and sterilised screwdriver (not because it's difficult to do – the width of the hole is better than a skewer).

Drop the figs into a large saucepan pan of boiling water and cook for 10 minutes. Drain and repeat this process at least twice.

Drain and cool. Once cooled, pack into a sterilised jar, packing tightly.

Combine the sugar, water, cinnamon stick, lemon zest and amaretto in a saucepan. Stir over medium heat to dissolve the sugar, then bring to the boil. Cook for 20–30 minutes, until it is thick and syrupy.

Pour most of the hot syrup over the figs. Put the lid on the jar and tip in different directions to try and release any trapped air bubbles, then add more syrup as required, to cover completely.

Allow to cool then store in the fridge for up to 2 weeks. Enjoy on ice cream, on top of ricotta on toast (see page 230), on porridge or rice pudding (see page 208).

Fig & Pear Mostarda

MAKES A 500ML JAR

⅓ cup (80ml) water
⅓ cup (80ml) apple cider vinegar
2 large pears
4 fresh figs
3 tbsp Dijon mustard
2 tbsp yellow mustard seeds
2 tbsp honey
1 tsp ground ginger

Mostarda simply means mustard in Italian. So this is actually a 'mostarda di frutta' – mustard fruit, which is a variation of a relish or chutney, using mustard for heat. Different areas of Italy use different fruits, but all have the mustard, so feel free to use different fruits from your garden throughout the season. I use pear and fig, because at that point in my garden that is what I have. Most fruits will work well. Apricots, peaches, quince, apples and citrus are all regularly used for this condiment. If my peach harvest is overwhelming this year I may use them for a pot or two of this.

This is a delicious condiment with contrasting sweet and savoury flavours. You can add a pinch of cayenne instead of ginger if you like. It's most delicious served with cold cut meats, in sandwiches and, of course, on cheese boards.

◆

Combine the water and vinegar in a saucepan. Peel, core and dice the pears (the smaller the pieces the better) and drop into the saucepan as they are done, to prevent discolouring.

Remove the stalks from the figs and dice into small pieces.

Add the remaining ingredients. Bring to the boil over medium-high heat, then reduce the heat to medium-low and simmer for 10–15 minutes until fruit has softened and the liquid is syrupy.

Let cool and then place in an airtight container or sterilised jar (see page 249) and keep in the fridge for up to 6 months.

Autumn

SEED SAVING

Seed saving was transformative to my gardening. It is actually very simple, but can become a whole genre of learning.

I started to understand the importance of seed saving long after learning to garden, especially about saving seed from plants that have already done well and I enjoyed growing in my garden. I came to it literally by force of nature and a little laziness, realising that leaving a seedhead to die naturally in place meant the plant would reappear by the dozen in the same spot. The biggest benefit to collecting seed from your own garden is not having to buy more seed next year. But you are also collecting seed from a plant that is happy, healthy and grows well in your garden, so there is a stronger chance these seeds will also do well. For me, knowing they are chemical free is also heartening.

Collecting fresh seed each year will give you a higher germination rate. Seeds that are a few years old or have been stored or handled badly may still germinate (I have been surprised many times by this), but it's so much easier with fresh seed. Over the years I have swapped seed with other gardeners and through this gained access to heirloom seeds that are not commercially available. Often heirloom varieties are more robust, and definitely come with a more interesting storyline.

Plants have many individual requirements when it comes to seed saving, so it is worth researching each plant individually. Things that you are looking for are cross-pollination and whether they will be true to type. The ones that are true to type is a good place to start, such as beans, tomatoes and most herbs. Every plant can be different though, for example dill and fennel will cross-pollinate and you may not know which plant you are going to get from the seeds you save. There are a lot of little idiosyncrasies, so I'm going to discuss a few of the main ways to save seeds, without going into huge depth.

Choose a variety that self-pollinates. Peas, beans, tomatoes, peppers, radishes and carrots are a good place to start. For best results save the seeds from your healthiest, most prolific plant. It is important to avoid a plant that is sick or unhealthy, or has just generally struggled in your garden as you don't want those poor traits to be repeated.

Let the fruit mature past the point you would usually pick it for the kitchen, then harvest the seeds. Let the seeds completely dry out to avoid any mould developing. Store in envelopes, small jars or containers and keep them in a dark, cool place away from temperature fluctuations, until you need them. Don't forget to label them!

A lot of herb flowers disperse seeds at the end of flowering, and some of these seeds are so tiny that attaching a little bag over the flowerhead is the only sure way of capturing the seed. This type of seed head will attract seed-eating birds to your garden, which offers another layer of diversity to your garden, but also competition for your seeds. An organza bag or even a carefully crafted paper 'envelope' attached to the flower head as it starts to die will collect plenty of seeds. A seedhead is nature's version of a birdfeeder – so unless you're looking for more flowers on a plant, let the seedhead remain and see who turns up for the seed.

Some seeds you can use right away. I have an ongoing supply of coriander, pansy and parsley with this method. Other seeds you will need to store until the next year, in order for the correct germination conditions for them. Each plant has its own set of rules around what works, so a little research is necessary for best results.

Here in New Zealand we are very fortunate not to have genetically modified plants, so saving seeds from anything in your garden is permissible. In a number of countries there are rules around proprietary ownership of certain strains of plants that have been bred, and they prohibit seed collection from those plants.

Buying seed will still provide a great outcome, but they will have come from a 'general population' of seed, not necessarily a plant that has proved itself over many years. Each gardener will have their own reason why something is the best. It could be a plant with the largest fruit, the earliest fruit (if they have short summers), it could be the most robust or disease-resistant, the most plentiful crop, or the best colour or flavour. By saving your own seed with your own criteria, you start to develop a garden that suits you and your own micro-climate of conditions, as well as preferences. The best advice I can give is to have a go, even if it is just one plant. Make sure to swap seeds with friends and neighbours. If your neighbour has strong, healthy plants, they are being cross-pollinated by birds and bees with your plants, so sharing those healthy seeds around your neighbourhood actually benefits your own garden too.

Eggplants

As soon as you have long, hot summer days it's time to plant your eggplants. Don't be tempted at the edge of spring, it really has to be Mediterranean-level summer days before you start planting these out in your garden. They need full sun for at least six hours of the day. Plenty of sunshine and water, perhaps near the strawberry patch if you have one!

I tend to grow the Black Beauty variety because I'm greedy and they are the biggest, with shiny dark skins. But there are plenty of varieties to choose from, in a range of colours and sizes. Some of the smaller Asian varieties can handle slightly cooler garden positions, so if that is your garden, it might be the place to start. There are so many more types to choose from than there used to be.

Growing eggplants in a terracotta pot on the deck is the best way I've found to start them off and get a little underway, while waiting for the days to heat up. You can actually quite successfully grow them fully in a pot without transferring them to the garden. They like the extra heat that a lot of other plants would shy away from, so if you have a full sun balcony give it a go.

They like the same sort of soil conditions as tomatoes: well fertilised with good drainage. Like a tomato plant, they will need a stake to grow up against, so pop this in early to avoid damaging roots later.

Try not to let your eggplant fruit get too big. There is an optimum size for picking. Obviously this will vary according to the variety, but they can get a bit woody and bitter if they are left on the plant for too long. Picking them also helps to encourage new blooms on the plant, so you will end up with more eggplants if you pick them regularly. Another thing to remember is that the plants are not particularly strong, so bigger and therefore heavier eggplants can easily break the stem.

The only real pest I've had with eggplants is the red spider mite, but I know that aphids can attack as well. I just blast them off with the hose every day for a few days in a row, which generally works.

Eggplants can be a bit hit and miss when it comes to pollination, so it is really helpful to attract some bees by having a few bee-friendly plants around them and avoiding the use of insecticides. If all else fails, a little paint brush will help move the pollen around. You'll know if your eggplants haven't been pollinated, because the flowers will just drop off the plant after flowering instead of turning into baby eggplants.

RECIPES

Eggplant Parmigiana

4 eggplants, cut into 1cm thick
   slabs
Olive oil, to drizzle
2 cups (500ml) pasta or Marinara
   sauce (see pages 102–3)
200g mozzarella, grated
50g parmesan, grated
Breadcrumbs (made from day-old
   bread), optional

This is one of the best uses for an eggplant harvest. Even allowing for an indulgent amount of cheese, it's a wonderful vegetarian meal on its own, served with a chunk of bread for mopping up the last delicious morsels. I have been known to add a layer of spinach or basil if I have either on hand in my garden. Make extra and freeze for those nights when you can't be bothered cooking – you will thank 'past you'. My house always smells amazing when I make this, and it hits a lot of nostalgic memories.

•

Preheat the oven to 190°C fan-forced and line a large baking tray with baking paper.

Lay the eggplant slices on the baking tray and drizzle with olive oil. Season with salt and pepper. Bake for about 20 minutes each side, until soft and lightly golden.

Arrange a layer of eggplant slices over the base of a 25cm × 20cm × 5cm deep baking dish. Top with a layer of pasta sauce, then mozzarella. Repeat the layers, finishing with sauce. Sprinkle with parmesan, and some breadcrumbs if you like.

Bake for 20 minutes, until the parmesan is golden and the sauce is bubbling.

•

NOTE: To make a BBQ version, cut the eggplants into wedges, drizzle with oil and cook on a covered BBQ until tender and lightly charred. Sprinkle with cheese and close the lid for a few minutes, to allow it to melt. Serve on a bed of warmed pasta sauce. Season with salt and pepper, and top with fresh basil leaves to serve.

Charred Eggplant Dip

2 large eggplants
2 garlic cloves, crushed
1 tsp lemon juice
2 tsp olive oil, plus extra to serve
Pinch of ground cumin
5–10 olives, finely chopped
Small handful fresh parsley,
   chopped
Chopped chilli, optional

A lot of my late summer, early-autumn veggies end up on the BBQ, purely because it's that time of year and, being a gardener, I tend to prefer being outside. My herb garden is right next to the BBQ in the courtyard, so often flavours end up together because of proximity and matching harvest times.

•

Roast the whole eggplants over an open flame (on the BBQ, on a gas burner on the cooktop, or under the grill), turning occasionally, until soft and charred. Split open and scoop out the soft flesh in the middle. You could also include some of the skin, chopped and mixed with the flesh. It adds favour, colour and texture.

Mix in the garlic, lemon juice, olive oil and ground cumin. Season with salt and pepper.

Spoon onto a platter or shallow bowl and sprinkle with the olives, parsley and chilli, if using. Drizzle with a little extra olive oil.

Great as a dip, or served under leafy green salads.

Grilled Eggplant in Oil

2 eggplants, cut into 1cm thick
    slices
2 garlic cloves, peeled
2 sprigs thyme (or more if you like)
10 black peppercorns
Extra virgin olive oil, to cover

I've only ever been able to grow enough eggplants to fill my freezer with premade parmigiana, but in season my 'local' sells them for a dollar each. So now I make this for antipasti platters – it's something that you can readily buy in any alimentari in Italy, but not so much in my local area. Zucchini can also be used, but not in the same jar. Zucchini (which become marrows when I'm tardy!) are more of a surplus problem in my garden.

•

Blanch the eggplant slices by dropping into a pot of boiling water for a minute or two. Remove, drain well, and pat dry with paper towel.

Heat the BBQ or a chargrill pan to high. Lightly oil the eggplant and cook for a minute or so each side, until golden.

Divide the eggplant slices between sterilised jars (see page 249) layering in the other ingredients as you go. Fill the jars with olive oil, or a lighter oil if you prefer. Jiggle the eggplant down with a fork a little to release any possible air pockets. Seal tightly.

These will keep for several months in a cool, dark pantry. Keep in the fridge for a week or two after opening.

NOTE: The fresher and better the quality of olive oil you use, the better this will taste.

Corn

The fact that I can buy corn cheaply from roadside stalls at the height of summer has slowed my enthusiasm for growing it myself. However, since it is one of those vegetables that is at its absolute best and sweetest the moment it is picked and goes downhill almost every hour from that point, it is absolutely worth doing so.

If you have the space in your garden, definitely make the most of it with a patch of corn. If you do grow your own corn, try eating one raw straight off the stalk. It is one of life's 'must have' food experiences that you will pretty much only get if you grow it yourself. The other commonly expressed view is to put a pot of water on to boil before you go to pick the corn. The cobs are also great cooked on the BBQ – an easy meal for a hot summer day.

You can start corn in your garden as seedlings, but it is just as easy to buy the packet of seeds and sow them directly once the soil has warmed a little in spring. Prepare the soil well, with plenty of compost and a layer of mulch before you start. Soak the seeds in tepid water for a few hours before planting. Plant the corn in clusters, so that proximity to each other helps with pollination. A sunny, sheltered spot and plenty of short waterings and you're on your way!

One of the best tips I can offer is to plant a small patch of corn every two weeks so that you have an ongoing supply.

If you are considering the 'green mulch' permaculture way of growing, the old-fashioned 'three sisters' method can work well here. It is also an extremely good use of space. Grow pumpkin or squash around the base of the plants to keep the soil from getting too hot and to keep the moisture in, and grow runner beans up the corn stems. This makes for a very symbiotic relationship between the plants.

Each tassel on the top of the corn is attached to a corn kernel and is pollinated individually. If you want to help with pollination on a still day, just gently tap each of the corn stalks, which will get the pollen moving.

Once the tassels turn brown and dry, your corn should be ready to pick.

Polenta & Corn Fritters

SERVES 4

360ml water
½ cup (85g) polenta
½ tsp salt
½ cup (80g) corn kernels (or your choice of small veggies)
¼ cup finely chopped spring onions, plus extra, to serve
1 tbsp finely chopped parsley
1 garlic clove, crushed
⅓ cup (50g) plain flour
¼ tsp baking powder
1 egg, lightly beaten
Vegetable oil, to deep fry
Mayonnaise, tomato, spring onion and coriander, to serve

This recipe has been a family favourite for years. Even though I use corn in the recipe, it is easy to sub in any other vegetables and often use this as a vehicle to use up less-favoured ones in our household. The Trojan horse for veggies, if you like. Once fried, the 'crust' tastes a lot like popcorn, and then it's just full of goodness. I always make too many, but they are great in the lunchbox the next day.

•

Bring the water to the boil in a saucepan over medium heat. Add the polenta and salt, and cook, stirring constantly, until thick.

Take off the heat and stir in the corn, spring onion, parsley and garlic. Leave to cool.

Sift the flour and baking powder over, and add the egg. Season with salt and pepper, and stir to combine.

Half fill a large saucepan with oil and heat over medium-high heat. Working a few at a time, scoop tablespoons of the mixture and gently drop into the hot oil. Cook for a few minutes, turning as needed, to a rich, golden brown colour. Drain on paper towel.

Drizzle with mayonnaise and top with chopped tomato, spring onion and coriander to serve, if you like.

NOTE: For extra pop, serve with your favourite tomato relish, or with yoghurt or sour cream as a dip.

Very Messy BBQ Corn

6 corn cobs, husks folded back,
  silk removed
Olive oil, to drizzle
2 limes
Sea salt, ground cumin and sweet
  paprika, to taste
Kewpie mayonnaise, to taste
Sweet chilli sauce, to taste
Parmesan, very finely grated,
  to taste
Spring onions, finely sliced, to taste
Fresh coriander, roughly chopped,
  to taste

This is so deliriously delicious and messy – a vegetarian 'spare ribs' experience! All of the toppings are to taste, so go light or heavy with your preferences. If you plan on doing this a few times over summer, allocate a pepper shaker for the spice mix, so that you have it permanently on hand (leave it by the BBQ!), to save time.

•

Preheat the BBQ or a chargrill pan on the stove to piping hot.

Drizzle the olive oil evenly over the corn and cook for about 10 minutes or until lightly charred, turning regularly to get a nice, even colouring.

Cut one of the limes into wedges. Finely grate the zest of the other one, then squeeze the juice.

In a small bowl, mix the salt and spices together.

Lay the corn on a platter and drizzle with the lime juice. Add the mayonnaise, a pinch of the spice mix for each of the cobs, then a drizzle of sweet chilli sauce. Top with a cloud of grated parmesan and the lime zest, spring onions and coriander.

All of this is in the quantities that you prefer, but lashings of mayonnaise is the key. Serve with the lime wedges to squeeze more juice over.

Capsicums

I've been growing capsicums for several years as annuals, but at the end of one season I didn't pull out the spent leafless stalk as I usually do. Come spring it bounced back to life, giving a good head start on all the plants I had grown from seed. Now I know that, in the right climate or spot in the garden, they are perennials – which just proves that there are always things to learn, and shortcuts to find.

That was a game changer for me. I promptly chose a spot and now have a 'pepper patch'. They are fairly low maintenance, and really start growing toward the end of spring. If you want a bushier plant, just pinch the tops out – tall lean plants will still do well, so it's not crucial.

Having a constant supply of capsicum over summer is amazing. Being able to gather one or two every few days, without having to do a lot of work, has definitely made this plant a favourite.

You can pick them when they are green or leave them to colour and ripen. The riper they are, the sweeter they will be. There seems to be very little interference from birds, so leaving them on the plant until they change colour poses no risk of missing out, and there is no need to net them.

One problem that can occur is that slugs love the leaves. You will need a deterrent (mine is to go out at night and collect them for the chickens) but there are a number of choices out there for slug prevention. It took me a while to realise that it was slugs causing the leaves to disappear – I had thought that the plants must be mildly deciduous!

Pepperonata Agrodolce

2 tbsp olive oil
1 garlic clove, sliced
4 capsicums, seeds removed, sliced
1 tbsp brown sugar (or honey)
1 tbsp balsamic vinegar
Capers, raisins, pitted olives and
    thyme sprigs, to taste (optional)

Agrodolce means sour (agro) and sweet (dolce). The balance of vinegar and sugar or honey works beautifully with the capsicums. This is a recipe that I always double, because when served cold on bruschetta the next day, it is even better.

•

Heat the oil in a large frying pan over medium heat and add the garlic. Add the capsicums and cook for about 10 minutes, stirring occasionally, until they start to soften.

Stir in the sugar and vinegar. Stir in the capers, raisins, olives and thyme, if using, then season with salt and pepper to taste.

Reduce heat to low and cook for a further few minutes, for juices to form and flavours to mingle. Transfer everything (including the pan juices) to a plate and serve just warm or at room temperature.

Keeps well for a few days in the fridge.

•

NOTE: It's nice to use a mixture of coloured capsicums because it looks pretty, but you can use whatever you have on hand.

Grilled Capsicum & Tomato Tart

1 tbsp olive oil, plus extra to drizzle
2 anchovy fillets
2 shallots, finely chopped
1 garlic clove, finely chopped
500g shortcrust pastry
150g gruyere, grated
4 tbsp chopped herbs (such as
   thyme, sage and oregano),
   plus extra, to serve
2 large heirloom tomatoes, sliced
3 large capsicums, cut into pieces
   and lightly chargrilled

This tart is almost better cold the next day than it is straight from the oven, making it perfect picnic food. Feel free to use puff pastry instead of shortcrust, but still leave a border around the edge so that you get a lovely crust.

•

Preheat the oven to 190°C fan-forced. Lightly grease a large baking tray.

Heat the olive oil in a frying pan over medium heat and cook the anchovies, shallots and garlic for a couple of minutes, until softened. Set aside to cool.

Roll out the pastry to a 30cm × 20cm rectangle and place onto the prepared tray. Spread the cooled anchovy mixture over, leaving a 2cm border around the edge.

Sprinkle with gruyere and herbs, then layer the tomato and capsicum on top, slightly overlapping.

Fold the edges of the pastry over to make a crust. Drizzle the topping with olive oil. Bake for 20–25 minutes, until pastry is golden.

Cool slightly and serve topped with a sprinkle of fresh herbs and cracked pepper.

Celery

Celery doesn't spring to mind as a hero ingredient like tomatoes or beans, but it's a quiet achiever – something I have been growing for years and use almost every day. I have a couple of celery plants that are several years old, and I continually pick a few stems at a time from them. Every time a recipe calls for an onion, I'll add a some finely diced celery as well. Every time I make a sandwich with lettuce or basil in it, I'll add a few young celery leaves plucked from the new growth. It's a mainstay of the kitchen and the garden – I have just never harvested it as a whole plant.

I had been warned off growing celery, as everything that I read led me to believe that it would be difficult, but it's not. Having said that, my plants never get the opportunity to become full-fledged supermarket size because we are gnawing away at them constantly. This is exactly how I like to use my garden, having a plant constantly supply me rather than swamp me once a year. Simply pluck the outer stems away from the plant and they make a handy lunch box item when you think you have nothing.

I grow celery in my salad garden area, which has finer soil and is watered slightly more often, and find that it thrives. Occasionally in the middle of summer the heat will cause the stems to become a little too stringy for eating raw, but finely sliced and cooked you would never know the difference. In fact at this time the flavour is a little stronger, so if you were going to dehydrate it for powder, this would be the time. It is at this point that I will either cut it back to ground level and water it so that it starts again, or let it go to seed, collect some for the spice drawer and let the rest naturally self-sow in the garden.

While it is on the 'dirty dozen' list for pesticides when grown commercially (one of the reasons I took a closer look at growing it) I haven't found it overly susceptible to pests. There is the odd snail but nothing too serious, and definitely nothing to warrant spraying. It is, however, susceptible to rust, often on the outer leaves. If it has just a few spots I use it anyway, as rust has no effect on it nutritionally. If the celery's leaves have turned brown and its stems are severely affected, I just remove all the affected stems and dispose of them, and find the plant recovers well.

These plants like a sunny but not too hot place in the garden (if anything, slightly cooler conditions). Morning or afternoon sun will be more than enough. They need regular watering and have shallow roots so a little water often is best.

Celery is not a hassle to grow from seed, although it does take a while to germinate. The easiest shortcut is to get a little set of seedlings from the garden centre for a few dollars. Pop them in different places in your garden, which helps to spread the harvest out a little as they will all grow at a slightly different rate. Also, if one of them is affected by rust or slugs you've still got the others. You'll also become aware of the best conditions for celery in your garden this way.

Winter

COMPOST

Any compost is better than no compost. It can get complicated, so start simple, maybe just with a leaf litter bin. I originally started with a worm farm before a compost bin, purely because it felt easier – just adding kitchen scraps.

I graduated to a black plastic compost bin and then, as I was running out of space and was reluctant to buy more plastic, my partner built an old-fashioned compost heap by my veggie patch out of old decking timber.

There is so much to know about compost that, when you start reading about it, it can seem like a huge commitment. I can safely say that any method I have attempted, even poorly, has happily provided compost long before I knew what I was doing – mother nature is great like that.

I have used what can best be described as the 'lasagne' method, which amounts to making nice layers of brown and green garden waste, and plant-based kitchen scraps. What often really happens is that I just dump stuff onto the pile. The thing I have been careful about is not including seed heads of plants I don't want back in the garden, but including ones that I don't mind reappearing as they often germinate in the compost. I figured I would rather have herbs and bee-friendly plants self sowing around my garden, taking up all the spare spaces until I needed them back, and that is what has happened. Borage, parsley, perpetual spinach and nasturtiums pop up everywhere around the garden, including the pathways.

The best compost has come from an old bin I rescued and put under a large tree. I dump all the leaf litter that collects on my driveway and deck in it, and nothing else. This is not by design, it's just the furthest bin from the house so it doesn't get anything else. The compost from that bin alone is pure black gold.

My next best discovery has been the in-ground worm towers for the planter boxes. They are super easy to use and really help to get nutrients down into a planter box in a slow-release fashion. When we moved in to our house, well over a decade ago, there was one planter box on the edge of the courtyard. I really struggled with keeping the soil rich – it was dry and lacked any form of nutrients, so nothing would grow well. I dug everything out and put a layer of manure and mulch in the bottom, and replaced half the soil with better soil from my garden, but it wasn't long before it was depleted again. I was actively looking for a solution and discovered this method of makeshift worm towers. They are a wide plastic tube (like an extra wide drainpipe) dug down into the planter box, which are used like a worm farm would be. I have three new planter boxes now all bursting with produce. One had eight tomato plants, basil and beans bursting out of it all summer long, and the other had asparagus that was big and lush. I then installed one in the greenhouse, tediously digging a long narrow hole to retrofit this worm tower, and the passionfruit plant that exploded forth has been astounding.

It goes to show even small-scale composting like using a worm tower can have big rewards in the garden. I'm at a point where I don't have enough kitchen scraps to go around, so the main compost pile misses out, as the expediency of the worm towers takes over.

If you have a balcony garden and there really is no other option, the best advice I have is to dump your banana peels in the blender and blitz with lots of water to make a nutritious plant smoothie. A little bit of seaweed, wild-gathered leaf litter (be sure it's not sprayed) – all the things that would make great compost can be added this way, in much smaller doses, when you water your plants.

Apples & Peaches

As an organic, spray-free gardener, this is my toughest customer, thanks entirely to coddling moth, and now guava moth. Don't be deterred, as the benefit of fresh fruit from your own trees far outweighs the problem.

I have a Granny Smith apple tree and they taste like nothing I can buy – the flesh is crisp and dense and the flavour is enough to remind me why I grow them.

If I were going to plant another tree, I would get one of those cleverly grafted apple trees with at least three of my favourite types of apples on it, maybe fruiting just slightly after one another. This way I would have a constant supply over a month or so.

The apple tree itself, like all fruit trees, requires a little pruning and they have been very tolerant of my beginner attempts. It really wasn't as hard as I had imagined, in fact they seem to be a very good learning medium and quite forgiving, or perhaps I was just lucky. First up – always cut away anything diseased or struggling. Next, trim anything that is rubbing on another branch (or anything nearby) and then those branches pointing back in toward the middle. After all of those have been attended to you can focus on pruning for shape. It helps to stand back from your tree and imagine where the branches that you leave will grow, a little like being a painter, stepping back for just a moment with a slightly raised brush for scale. It is important to use pruning paste on the cuts, to keep them clean. This can just be a mixture of beeswax and olive oil.

If you are planting a new tree – even though they are available all year round – the best times to plant are late autumn and early spring. Try to choose a sheltered but sunny spot so that the wind doesn't blow all your blossoms off in spring.

In fact, most fruit trees are at their prettiest in spring. In hindsight, I should have planted mine where they could be seen best from a window in the house, purely to get the full impact of their blossoms and early growth. Because fruit trees are long-lived, choosing where to put them is important. They want something very middle of the road – not too try and not too soggy.

As summer rolls on, you can help them thrive by mulching around their base to lower the ground temperature and help keep moisture in. Watering in the early morning or evening is most effective as it gives the tree a longer period of access to the water before the heat of the day removes it.

The trees themselves provide a little shade for smaller plants – I keep a few potted herbs under mine.

Growing fruit trees from seed is not really feasible, as they don't necessarily replicate the fruit, but if you like a lucky dip, by all means go for it.

Apple Doughnuts

1 cup (150g) self-raising flour
2 tbsp sugar
Pinch of salt
2 eggs
½ cup (125ml) milk
1 tbsp Marsala (optional)
3 large apples, diced into 1cm
cubes
Vegetable oil, to deep-fry
Honey, icing sugar or cinnamon
sugar, to serve

This is sometimes a weekend brunch, and sometimes a dessert. They are also really delicious with bananas or peaches in them. It is better with just one type of fruit in it, and apple was the original Italian recipe. I just came up with the other versions when I had fruit that I needed to use up – often the best recipes are found this way.

•

Mix the flour, sugar and salt in a large bowl. Mix the eggs, milk and Marsala (if using) together, then add to the dry ingredients and stir to combine. Gently fold in the apple.

Half-fill a large saucepan with oil and heat over medium-high heat. Working a few at a time, gently drop large spoonfuls of mixture into the hot oil.

Cook for about 2 minutes, turning halfway through cooking, until crisp and golden brown all over. Drain on paper towels.

Drizzle with honey, or dust with icing sugar or cinnamon sugar to serve.

Spiced Apple Cake

SERVES 12

4 apples, quartered, cored, but
    not peeled
2 eggs
2 cups (440g) sugar
2 tsp bicarbonate of soda
2 tsp ground allspice
250g butter, at room temperature,
    chopped
2 cups (300g) plain flour
1 tsp ground cinnamon
Ice cream and caramel sauce,
    to serve

CINNAMON CRUMBLE
½ cup (110g) brown sugar
½ cup (45g) rolled oats
1 tsp ground cinnamon
25g butter

This recipe hails from my mother's café, Eliza's Pantry. It's super simple and uses four apples with their skin on. The apples don't have to be at their best, it's a little like a banana bread recipe for apples. They can be rescued because no one is inclined to eat them, and turned into something delicious – but the best part is that it is all just mixed up in a food processor then baked.

•

Preheat the oven to 180°C fan-forced. Grease a 23cm springform tin and line with baking paper.

To make the crumble, combine the ingredients in a food processor and process until crumbly. Transfer to a bowl and set aside.

For the cake, place the apples into the food processor and process until finely chopped. Add the remaining ingredients and process for 1 minute. Pour into the prepared tin and sprinkle with the topping.

Bake for 1–1¼ hours, until a skewer inserted into the centre comes out clean. Cool in the pan for 10 minutes, then transfer to a wire rack to cool completely.

Serve with ice cream, caramel sauce, or both.

Apple Slaw

1 Granny Smith apple, julienned
3 tbsp sliced almonds, toasted
2 cups finely shaved cabbage or
    Brussels sprouts
½ carrot, julienned
1 cup torn herb leaves (such as
    mint, coriander and parsley)
¼ red onion, finely sliced

LEMON DRESSING
100ml lemon juice
50ml white balsamic
1 tbsp honey
100ml light olive oil
Pinch of sea salt flakes

I love the freshness an apple brings to a slaw. When my Granny Smith tree was heaving apples and my freezer already had a load of stewed apple for winter, I started adding them to everything. They were scattered among the roast veggies on roast nights, sliced and tucked into muffins, or even slivered and added to grilled cheese sandwiches. The other outcome has been that every coleslaw now has apple in it!

·

To make the dressing, whisk the ingredients together, or shake vigorously in a jar. Alternatively, you could use the apple dressing on page 192.

Lightly toss all the salad ingredients together until evenly mixed. Toss with dressing to taste.

·

NOTE: If you are substituting the apple type, choose a crisp rather than sweet variety.

Apple Dressing

2 apples, grated
1½ celery sticks, very finely diced
1 onion, very finely diced
2 tbsp toasted sesame seeds
600ml rice vinegar
200ml soy sauce
1 tsp sesame oil

One of my all-time favourites to have on hand. I use it more as a sauce than an actual vinaigrette. A light drizzle on a venison tataki is bliss. It lasts for ages and is very moreish – you will find yourself dolloping it over a fresh garden salad regularly. My apple tree has always overloaded me with stewed apple and apple cake variations, so this way of using them up is a nice relief.

Combine all the ingredients in a jar and seal the lid tightly. Shake well to combine. Season with salt and sugar to taste.

Store in the fridge for up to 2 months. Shake to recombine before using.

Apple Cider Vinegar

4 apple skins and cores (seeds
    removed)
⅓ cup (75g) sugar
2 cups (500ml) warm filtered water

*Apple cider vinegar is fairly cheap to buy, but because this is literally
made from scraps, it's a great way to reduce waste.*

•

Combine the apple skins and cores in a sterilised jar (see page 249).
Add the sugar and water. Cover the top with some muslin to prevent
fruit flies (not an airtight lid).

Place into a cool dark pantry or cupboard for 2 weeks.

Strain out the apple skins and cores. Seal with a lid and put away for
another 2 weeks before using.

Use in salad dressings, shrubs, chutneys and marinades (see Garden-
Inspired recipes beginning on page 247). Apple cider vinegar with
honey has some definite health benefits and is great in a hot drink.
Add a few warm-toned spices (such as cinnamon and ginger) and
even some orange zest.

Peach Cobbler

SERVES 6–8

1kg peaches, roasted, stones
    removed
1 small lemon, zest finely grated,
    juiced
2 tbsp brown sugar
4 eggs
⅔ cup (150g) sugar
1 tsp vanilla extract (or maple
    extract)
¾ cup (110g) plain flour
1 tsp baking powder
Pinch of salt
½ cup (120g) finely chopped
    nuts, such as walnuts or pecans
    (optional)
Cinnamon sugar, to sprinkle
Ice cream or cream, to serve

I'm not sure if this is strictly a cobbler, as it is more of a sponge or cake batter on the top of the fruit. It came about as a shortcut way to use up a surplus of fruit – primarily from the peach tree, who dumps all her ripe peaches in the space of a week (literally several kilos a day). They are small white peaches that bruise easily, so they need to be used quickly before they deteriorate. This recipe is easily converted to use any fruit, such as plums, pears or apples, or even rhubarb. It can be jazzed up with a few nuts or herbs to make it your own. The fruit can be raw or cooked, and if you have some preserved fruit this is a great way to use it. I like to roast the peaches before making the cobbler, simply because I'm lazy. Roasting softens the skin, so I don't have to peel them, and the stones come out easily. I would use the same technique on any other small stone fruit, but would just use rhubarb or pears raw. It's a forgiving recipe.

•

Preheat the oven to 190°C fan-forced.

Spread the fruit over the base of a deep 8 cup capacity baking dish. Add a squeeze of lemon juice and the zest, then sprinkle over the brown sugar.

Use electric beaters to beat the eggs in a large bowl until foamy. Gradually add the sugar, beating constantly. Beat in the vanilla. Fold in the flour, baking powder and salt, then the nuts if using.

Spoon mixture over the fruit, and sprinkle the top with cinnamon sugar. Bake for 15–20 minutes or until the top springs back when gently touched.

Serve hot with ice cream, and cold with cream the next morning for breakfast.

Citrus

In Italy citrus, particularly lemon, is used everywhere. Lemon granita or gelato, limoncello, lemon cakes and desserts, even lemon pasta. There are many other citrus types to explore though, and they are often interchangeable in recipes. Lime, mandarin, grapefruit, orange, blood orange, makrut, finger lime, tangelo – interestingly most of the varieties we have now come directly from the pomelo, mandarin and citron. All the different attributes of these citrus, and more, have come through different combinations of these three over many generations of cross pollination. The exception is the finger lime, which is an Australian native. A little research, or a wander around your neighbourhood checking what's growing well in neighbours' yards, will help you decide the perfect citrus for your garden.

Citrus prefer sunshine, lots of feeding and a frost-free position. Feeding can consist of lawn clippings, animal manure or blood and bone, as they are not particularly picky.

All citrus can be very heavy producers in the right conditions and the thing I enjoy most is that you don't have to harvest all the fruit at once. You can 'graze' the tree, just taking what you need each day. I have always enjoyed being able to grab a lemon or lime as I need one in the kitchen.

A good range of trees are in my garden now as a citrus grove. If space is going to be an issue, just choose your favourite, the one you will use the most.

Lemon trees are fairly common in most backyards and often survive without much attention, producing fruit for a large part of the year. Limes are just as easy to grow, so if this is something you use a lot of then adding another tree isn't going to increase your garden workload. They are a fruit that gets a little pricey to buy, so it may be worth putting one next to the lemon tree. Mandarin varieties can fruit at slightly different times. I have two now – an easy peel satsuma and an Encore – ensuring a longer harvest period.

If you are in a colder climate you may get away with a warm corner of the garden, near a fence, but in the outright cold, a pot would be your best bet. Many varieties are happy in a pot, just make sure your soil is free draining.

As far as pruning is concerned, there isn't a lot of work to do. Just prune away anything that is dead or diseased, and then provide a little 'shape' to it if you want. They are very forgiving if you don't get around to it.

In summer you will need to keep an eye on watering. The root system is shallow, which is why they are fine in pots, so they can dry out easily with too many hot days in a row.

My Italian grandparents had a large lemon tree at the back corner of their garden in Nelson. It was next to the fence on one side and the neighbour's glasshouse on the other. This made for the perfect microclimate, and it absolutely thrived. It was large, or maybe I was little and I am remembering it in comparison, but I did fit under it easily.

Most citrus can be grown from seed, but it takes a while and as most citrus are already hybrids you may not get an exact replica of the fruit you have taken the seed from. A commercial grower will graft fruit onto stronger root stock in order to replicate the plant exactly, and they will be a few years old already before you buy them, so these are the best bet.

Citrus Zest Powder

If you want to make the most of your citrus, use a vegetable peeler to take the zest off the fruit, avoiding as much of the white pith as possible. Put on a baking tray in the oven overnight – the oven should be turned off but still warm from cooking dinner. Or use a dehydrator if you have one. Once the peel is dry you can blitz it to a powder and keep in an airtight container. Great for adding zesty flavour to your recipes when citrus is out of season – use ½ tsp powder for every 1 tsp zest required.

RECIPES

Lemon Granita

1½ cups (375ml) water
1 cup (220g) sugar
Finely grated lemon zest (see note)
¾ cup (185ml) lemon juice

If you have a lot of limes or grapefruit, go right ahead and swap the lemons out. Mandarins would also be delicious. Lemon granita is often served with espresso coffee on a hot summer afternoon in southern Italy, and is an equally refreshing way to cool down anywhere in the world.

•

Combine the water and sugar in a saucepan over medium heat. Stir to dissolve the sugar then bring it to the boil and simmer for a few minutes. Remove from the heat and cool completely.

Whisk in the lemon zest and juice. Pour into a shallow tray and place into the freezer. After about one hour, bring it out and scratch the ice crystals apart with a fork. Return to the freezer. Scrape again after one hour and return to the freezer. It should resemble a slushy, but will be a bit firmer.

When you are ready to serve, scrape repeatedly with a fork until it resembles fluffy crushed ice.

•

NOTE: Zest adds an intense lemon flavour, so add as much or as little as you prefer.

Lemon Coconut Loaf

2 lemons
2 tbsp brown sugar
2 cups (300g) self-raising flour
1 cup (80g) desiccated coconut
1 cup (220g) sugar
1 cup (250ml) milk

This is one of my mother's recipes from her café. It's so simple that I would often make it on a Sunday night when I had nothing baked for school lunches for the upcoming week. It can be made with equal success without the lemon slice and brown sugar layer, if you want to skip a step, and is also delicious using any other citrus. It really is one of those pantry basics recipes, which take minimal effort, but don't look that way! I was generally baking something a day or so later to replace it, as it disappears so quickly, but I learnt to cut the loaf up into slices or squares myself to make it last a little longer (others in the house would cut 'slices' that resembled the size of a lamington!).

•

Preheat the oven to 160°C and line a 20 x 10cm (base measurement) loaf tin with baking paper.

Wash the lemons, then thinly slice one and cut the slices in half. Finely grate the zest from the other lemon, then squeeze the juice.

Mix the brown sugar and lemon juice together and spread evenly over the base of the loaf tin. Arrange the lemon slices over the sugar mixture, overlapping very slightly as they will shrink a little while baking.

Fold all the remaining ingredients (including lemon zest) together gently, until just combined. Pour the mixture into the loaf tin and spread out to an even layer.

Bake for 1 hour, or until a skewer inserted into the centre comes out clean. Cool in the pan for 10 minutes, then turn out onto a wire rack to cool completely.

Lemon & Almond Biscotti

2½ cups (375g) plain flour
1 tsp bicarbonate of soda
3 eggs
1 cup (220g) sugar
Pinch of salt
Finely grated zest of 1 lemon
180g raw almonds (not blanched)
1 tbsp milk

Biscotti are wonderful to have on hand to serve with creamy desserts or gelato, or to dunk in your coffee or grappa!

•

Preheat the oven to 180°C fan-forced. Line a large baking tray with baking paper.

Sift the flour and bicarb into a bowl. Use electric beaters to beat 2 of the eggs, sugar, salt and lemon zest together. Add the flour mixture and almonds to the egg mixture and fold together until combined.

Gather the dough into a ball then roll into a log about 35cm long and 10cm wide. Place onto the baking tray. Whisk the remaining egg with milk using a fork and brush over the dough. Bake for 30 minutes, until golden.

Keeping oven heated, remove logs and cool them a few minutes, until safe to handle. Cut into as thin slices as possible. Arrange on the baking tray and return to the oven for 10 minutes, until slices are crisp and dry.

Store in an airtight container for up to 1 week.

•

NOTE: You can swap the almonds for hazelnuts or pistachios, and use orange or lime zest in place of the lemon zest.

Pizza Dolce

PASTRY
120g butter, chopped
120g sugar
1 egg, plus 2 egg yolks
280g plain flour
½ tsp baking powder
Cinnamon sugar, to sprinkle

LEMON FILLING
350ml milk
1 cup (250ml) cream
140g sugar
90g plain flour
3 egg yolks
Finely grated zest of 1 lemon
   (more if you really like lemon)

CHOCOLATE FILLING
350ml milk
1 cup (250ml) cream
140g sugar
90g plain flour
20g cocoa powder
1 tsp ground cinnamon
½ tsp vanilla extract

Nonna made this for anyone who requested it, but did not share the recipe easily. You had to have participated in the making to know how. Its page in her recipe book is so worn at the corner that you can no longer read the ingredients. Over the years I made it, there was a stage where it failed a couple of times. It dawned on me one day when I was making ricotta that the milk Nonna used was always full of cream that you had to dislodge from the top of the glass bottle. So I now use a combination of milk and cream.

This needs to be made in advance to fully cool down, and tastes better as a stolen slice the next morning, with espresso, for breakfast.

•

To make the pastry, use electric beaters to beat the butter and sugar until pale and creamy. Beat in the egg and yolks. Sift the flour and baking powder over and use a knife to mix to a dough. Gather the dough into a ball, cover and chill while you make the filling.

To make the lemon filling, combine the ingredients in a saucepan. Whisk slowly over low heat until thickened, then continue cooking and whisking for another 2 minutes, until it reaches a porridge-like consistency. Pour into a bowl, cover and leave to cool.

Make the chocolate filling the same way (except add the vanilla at the end of cooking time), then pour into a bowl, cover and leave to cool.

Preheat the oven to 160°C fan-forced. Roll out ⅔ of the pastry and use to line a 22cm springform tin. Roll out the remaining pastry to use as a lid. Refrigerate until needed (it's easier to handle when slightly chilled).

To assemble, spread the chocolate filling over the pastry base. Top with the lemon filling and gently smooth the surface with the back of a spoon. Lay the pastry lid on top, seal the edges together and cut away any excess dough.

Bake for 30–40 minutes, until the pastry is golden brown and fully cooked on top. You will see it start to come away from the edges of the cake tin slightly.

Sprinkle with cinnamon sugar, then set aside to cool in the tin for about 20 minutes. Remove from the tin and allow to cool completely.

Italian Lemon & Ricotta Doughnuts

MAKES ABOUT 12

1 cup (240g) ricotta (see page 230)
3 eggs
¼ cup (55g) sugar
½ tsp vanilla essence
1¼ cups (185g) plain flour
2 tsp baking powder
Finely grated zest of 1 lemon
Vegetable oil, to deep-fry
Icing sugar, lemon syrup or honey,
    to serve

This is a simple everyday Italian recipe. They are just as delicious as a yeast-based doughnut, but without the fuss. We often have them for a weekend brunch, but they should possibly be dessert!

•

Half-fill a large saucepan with oil and heat over medium-high heat.

Gently mix the ricotta, eggs, sugar, vanilla, flour, baking powder and lemon zest together until evenly combined.

Working in batches, gently drop large spoonfuls of mixture into the hot oil and deep-fry until deep golden brown.

Drain on paper towel, cool slightly and dust with icing sugar, or drizzle with lemon syrup or honey to serve.

Mandarin-scented Rice Pudding

SERVES 4

75g short grain rice, washed
  and drained
330ml milk
160ml cream
½ vanilla bean pod, seeds scraped
1 tbsp finely grated mandarin zest
75ml condensed milk
40g unsalted butter
1 mandarin, deseeded and finely
  sliced (optional)
1 tbsp raw sugar (or honey)

A delicious variation to this dish is to add chopped rhubarb to the base of the dish before you add everything else in – it cooks just perfectly.

•

Preheat the oven to 150°C fan-forced. Spread the rice over the base of a four 1½ cup capacity ovenproof dishes, or one 6 cup capacity ovenproof dish.

Combine the milk, cream, vanilla seeds and mandarin zest in a saucepan over medium-low heat. The moment it simmers take it off the heat and stir in the condensed milk and butter, then pour over the rice.

Bake uncovered for 1 hour, until the rice is tender. Garnish with mandarin slices, if using. Sprinkle with the raw sugar and grill briefly until golden.

Mandarin & Fennel Salad

SERVES 2

1 fennel bulb
4 mandarins
Baby celery leaves, calendula petals
    and fried capers, optional
Walnuts, lightly toasted, to taste

ZESTY ORANGE DRESSING
1 tsp wholegrain mustard
1 tsp finely grated orange zest
1 tsp honey
¼ cup (60ml) orange juice
¼ cup (60ml) olive oil
2 tbsp apple cider vinegar

These two ingredients are often ready in the garden at the same time – mid to end of winter – when a lot of other produce is either finished or not ready yet. Between them they are packed with flavour vitality that will make you think it is spring.

Clean the fennel bulb, remove the outer leaf if it is damaged, and cut the woody base off. Trim off the stems and fronds, keeping some fronds for garnish. Cut the bulb in half from top to bottom across the narrow width and then finely slice, using a mandolin if you have one. Place into a large bowl of cold water while you prepare the rest of the ingredients.

Peel the mandarins and slice into nice rounds.

To make the dressing, whisk the ingredients together, or place in a jar with a lid and shake well. Season with salt and pepper to taste. Any leftover dressing will easily keep for a week or so in the fridge. Shake to blend before each use.

Arrange the fennel and mandarin slices onto a plate and garnish with the reserved fennel fronds and the baby celery leaves, calendula petals and fried capers, if using.

Drizzle with dressing and sprinkle with the walnuts.

NOTE: Oranges and mandarins are interchangeable in both salad and dressing, if you like.

Citrus Slice

1 cup (80g) desiccated coconut
125g plain biscuits, crushed
1 cup (250ml) condensed milk
Finely grated zest of 1 orange,
    plus a little extra, for garnish
Finely grated zest of 1 lime, plus
    a little extra, for garnish
125g butter, melted
1 cup (160g) icing sugar
Orange juice, as needed
Petal sugar (see page 56), for
    garnish

When I travelled to Nelson for the school holidays to stay with Nonna, she always filled the cookie tin with our favourite goodies. Not just my favourites, but of my friends in Nelson too, so there would be a curated selection of cookies with something for everyone. This was one of mine. It is made with orange (or mandarin for me), but is equally delicious made with lemon.

•

Combine the coconut, crushed biscuits, condensed milk and grated zest in a mixing bowl. Pour the melted butter over and mix well. Press into a 20cm square tin.

Place into the fridge and chill for at least 30 minutes.

Mix the icing sugar with a little orange juice until you reach a fairly stiff consistency. You can always add more icing sugar or juice, depending if it is too wet or dry. Spread over the slice and garnish with a little orange and lime zest, as well as petal sugar if you are using. Leave to set in the fridge.

•

NOTE: For a grown-up version, replace the zest with 1 tsp coffee essence, reduce the coconut to ½ cup and add 1 cup chopped walnuts. Use a dash of coffee as the liquid in the icing, and garnish with chopped walnuts.

Limoncello

4 lemons
1½ cups (375ml) vodka
3 cups (750ml) water
1¼ cups (275g) sugar

I've drunk too much limoncello in Italy, but also not spent enough time in Italy drinking limoncello. One of my most memorable episodes was in my twenties on the deck of a tiny restaurant in Stromboli, overlooking Strombolicchio in the Tyrrhenian Sea. I think we had arrived for a late morning espresso and then lingered so long it became appropriate to abandon the espresso drinking for chilled limoncello. A hot sunny afternoon in mid-summer, on a tiny island where time stands still, the heat offset by an ocean breeze and the chilled limoncello … perfection.

•

Wash the lemons well. Use a small sharp knife or a vegetable peeler to remove the skin in strips, with as little white pith as possible.

Place into a glass jar with the vodka. Seal with a lid and store in a cool dark place for 4–6 weeks.

Combine the sugar and water in a saucepan and stir over low heat to dissolve the sugar. Set aside to cool.

Strain the lemon skins from the vodka, then stir the vodka into the sugar syrup. Place into a bottle and seal. Limoncello is best kept in the freezer and served cold.

•

NOTE: If you are using commercially grown lemons, wash well in warm water and rub with a tea towel to remove any wax.

Amaretto

2 cups (500ml) water
1 cup (220g) sugar
½ cup brown sugar
1 tsp honey
1 vanilla bean, split, seeds scraped
2 cups (500ml) vodka
2 tbsp almond extract

Amaretto is a favourite in Italy. Originally from Saronno, the commonly known brand, Disaronno, means 'of Saronno' just as my name, DiMattina, means 'of morning'. True amaretto was not made from almonds at all, but rather peach or apricot pips, and wasn't always as sweet as it is now – if you ever try Amaro in Italy, you will find it wildly bitter! This version is easy to make and works well for baking, as well as in cocktails for its lovely almond/marzipan flavour.

•

Combine the water, sugars, honey and vanilla bean and seeds in a small saucepan and stir over low heat until sugar has dissolved. Remove from the heat and set aside to cool completely.

Stir in the vodka and almond extract, and remove vanilla bean.

Place into a bottle and seal. Store in a cool dark cupboard. Serve over ice, always!

Nutella Liqueur with Orange Zest

1 cup (250ml) milk
1 cup (250ml) cream
1 cup (300g) Nutella
1 tsp finely grated orange zest
½ cup (125ml) vodka

Orange zest gives a lovely lift to this creamy Italian liqueur. It's delicious served chilled, though you might like to add a dash to your coffee.

•

Place the milk, cream, Nutella and orange zest in a heavy-based saucepan over low heat. Stir until combined then remove from the heat the moment this happens (you do not need to boil or simmer). Set aside to cool.

Strain the mixture to remove the zest. Stir in the vodka. Place into a bottle and seal. Store in the fridge for up to 3 weeks.

Old-fashioned Mandarin-ade

MAKES ABOUT 1 LITRE

3 mandarins
80g sugar (or honey), to taste
1 litre chilled water
Mint, for garnish

This recipe is on high rotation in our house and makes great use of damaged fruit, as the quantities are flexible. I often mix and match the citrus – if there is a lime hanging around the fruit bowl, it will go in with the mandarins – but will also add herbs like mint and lemon balm.

Leaving the skin on, cut the mandarins in half crossways and remove the seeds, then cut each piece into quarters. Place in a blender with the sugar and half of the water. Blitz a few times. Add the remaining water and repeat.

Strain into a jug and serve over ice with mint.

Avocados

Fun fact: avocados are berries!

These are the golden goose of the suburban garden, often grown from a pip on the windowsill in the kitchen. If you are serious about having one in the garden, I would recommend that you grab a grafted one from a garden store. While there is a chance your avocado will fruit if grown from seed, there is also a chance that it won't. They often do not reproduce 'true to type', and the wait for the first fruit is several years! That doesn't mean to say you shouldn't pop those windowsill ones in the garden – I definitely would if I had the space, but for a guaranteed outcome, the grafted tree will save on heartache.

This evergreen tree is a gem to have in the garden, although it doesn't like frost much, particularly when it is young. If you are committed, you can choose a very sheltered spot and cover it with frost cloth for the first couple of winters, then you should be okay.

They require free-draining soil and regular watering, particularly during summer. They flower in spring and the fruit will develop over the summer and be ready on the tree from as early as May. This is where the 'gem' rating comes in, as they do not finish ripening until you pick them. So if you have a large harvest, they can be left on the tree until you are ready. I have overlapped harvests this way and had a year-round supply of avo on toast! The longer you leave them, the richer, oilier and nuttier the flavour, but the birds will also eventually figure this out.

Pick a few every few days, then allow 10 days or so (more in winter, less in summer) to ripen.

The tree is best when pruned, as it can grow quite tall. It is easier to harvest if you manage the growth by pruning. The tree will send out new branches quickly, and still fruit really well.

They can self pollinate, as each bundle of flowers is both male and female, that open and close at different times of the day. A second tree would be helpful, but this requires careful research, as there are two types, which are literally known as Type A and Type B. Type A have flowers that open as a female in the morning of day one, close, and open as a male in the afternoon of day two. Type B open as female flowers in the afternoon of day one, and as male flowers in the morning of day two. If you can find a Type A and Type B that flower at a similar time of year, this will provide the best outcome. I have just one tree and still have plenty of fruit, with the help of lots of pollinating insects. So even in sub-optimal conditions there are enough avocados for me to consider the tree an amazing garden asset.

RECIPES

Avocado Green Goddess Dressing

MAKES ABOUT 375ML

1 ripe avocado, flesh scooped out
⅓ cup (150g) raw cashews
Small handful parsley, to taste
Small handful mint, to taste
Small handful chives, to taste
1 garlic clove
½ cup (140g) plain yoghurt
  (or sour cream)
2 tbsp olive oil
2 tbsp lime juice
2 tsp capers in brine, drained
1 tsp brine from the capers

This is a very delicious and also nutritious alternative salad dressing. You can make it a little thicker if you like by adding more avocado, and serve it as a dip – which I highly recommend. It's a great use of avocados that are a little too soft to slice and use in the actual salad.

•

Combine all the ingredients in a blender, and blend to the texture that you prefer. Season with salt and pepper to taste.

Serve drizzled over salad leaves.

Spring Green
Avocado Salad

200g shelled broad beans
100g feta
4 sprigs mint, coarsely chopped
2 avocados, diced
200g watercress or rocket (or a
    combination of both)

The thing about gardening is the creativity of using what you have from the garden. Look to use whatever comes into season at the same time – tomatoes and basil have been an Italian staple forever for this reason. In my garden, avocados and broad beans happen to do their thing together in late winter/early spring, leading to this little winter salad that should be shared.

•

Lightly blanch the broad beans by cooking in a saucepan of boiling water for 1 minute, then draining and dropping into a bowl of iced water. Drain well. Peel the skins from any larger beans, but if they are small and tender you can leave them on.

Lightly mash with the feta and mint, then toss with the avocado.

Spoon over a bed of watercress and/or rocket. Season with sea salt to serve.

Not Your Average Avocado Toast

2 avocados, flesh chopped
200g cream cheese, chopped
Handful chives, to taste
Handful coriander, to taste
2 limes, zest finely grated, juiced
½ cup (80g) pine nuts, toasted
Toasted sourdough bread, to serve

This is wonderful on sourdough toast with diced ripe tomato. Top with coriander leaves and sprinkle with a few more toasted pine nuts.

•

Combine all the ingredients (except the pine nuts) in a food processor and process until smooth. Add the pine nuts and process in a couple of short bursts so that some texture is left in the nuts.

Pile onto toast to serve.

Avocado & Lime Ice Blocks

SERVES 6

2 ripe avocados, flesh scooped out
3 limes, zest finely grated, juiced
400ml can coconut milk
1 cup (250ml) maple syrup
⅓ cup (80ml) water

My lime tree and avocado tree are both full of fruit in winter, so this was almost a way of preserving them. It's a little out of season for ice blocks, but this will transport you to spring for a moment.

•

Combine all the ingredients in a blender and blend until smooth. If you have an ice cream machine, add the mixture and make according to the machine instructions.

If you do not have an ice cream machine, pour the mixture into ice cube trays, reserving about 100ml of the mixture in the fridge until needed. Freeze the mixture in the trays.

Combine the frozen mixture and the chilled mixture in a blender and blend until smooth. Transfer to an ice block mould and place into the freezer until firm.

If you cannot wait, however, you can also serve immediately.

Staples

This is a collection of recipes that I use all the time. They provide a base, then the garden pops up with a vegetable or two and suddenly it becomes a meal. Whether it's homemade mascarpone with fruit, or pasta and gnocchi with whatever vegetable is ready from the garden, the combinations are endless and always an absolute delight. You could just buy all these things, but the satisfaction of making them yourself is wonderful.

Fresh Ricotta

MAKES ABOUT 200G

2 cups (500ml) full cream milk
   (not homogenised)
200ml cream
Pinch of sea salt (must be
   non-iodised)
20ml fresh lemon juice

RICOTTA ON TOAST

Fresh ricotta on sourdough toast is
so good, and these are a few of the
toppings I like to add:

Poached asparagus & lemon zest

Grilled tomatoes

Stewed rhubarb (see page 134)

Figs & honey

This recipe was the start of my journey with Nonna's recipe book. A milestone moment, as it provided a journey I wasn't expecting. It was just a scrawled, rather scant, list of ingredients (in gallons), scribbled on the inside back cover, with no method.

I've made ricotta so many times that I decided to enter it into the New Zealand Cheese awards, where it was judged champion cheese in 2014 by Australia's and New Zealand's top cheesemakers. So this recipe and I have a wonderful history together.

Traditionally ricotta would have been made with the leftover whey from making another cheese (ricotta means 'twice cooked'). In Italian life, it has always been important not to waste anything. The lemon juice would create a second curd from the whey of the first cheese. The whey could also be used as a base for soup or in baking, or fed to the animals as a treat.

Ricotta is the easiest of all cheeses to make at home, and fresh ricotta is so much fluffier and richer than bought ricotta. It's hard to resist slathering it on toast with fresh fruit or tomatoes on top!

•

Combine the milk, cream and salt in a heavy-based saucepan over low heat. Place a candy thermometer into the pan. Heat slowly, stirring gently just occasionally. When the temperature reaches 80°C remove pan from the heat and add the lemon juice. I always add just a little at a time and swirl it in gently before I add a little more. Just as you see the mixture start to separate, stop adding juice and let it sit for a while. The amount of lemon juice needed can vary, depending on the milk, so as long as you are adding just a little at a time it will be fine.

Place a colander over a bowl, and line the colander with cheesecloth or muslin. Pour the mixture into the colander and set aside for about an hour to drain naturally (don't press or squeeze it). You could also put it in the fridge overnight if you would like a drier curd.

The solid part is the curd (the ricotta cheese), and the liquid is the whey. Keep both the curd and whey in separate containers in the fridge until needed.

•

NOTE: If you like, use a double boiler, which will ensure that the mixture heats slowly.

Mascarpone

1 litre cream
2 tbsp lemon juice

Mascarpone is a delicious thick Italian cream, usually used in desserts, but often found on cereal and porridge at our place.

•

Place the cream into a heatproof bowl. Stand the bowl over a saucepan of simmering water on low heat. Slowly heat the cream to 82°C (use a candy thermometer to test), then stir in the lemon juice. Stir gently until the mixture thickens.

Remove from the heat and leave to cool. Cover and refrigerate overnight (it becomes even thicker when chilled).

Line a sieve with muslin or strong paper towel and place over a large bowl. Scoop the thickened cream into the sieve, leaving behind liquid accumulated in the base of the bowl. Place in the fridge to drain for several hours, until it has reached your desired texture.

Transfer to an airtight container and keep in the fridge for up to a week.

Verjuice

2 bundles unripe (but full-sized)
    green grapes
Pinch of citric acid (optional)

Verjuice (or verjus) is an old recipe. Actually it is barely even a recipe, just literally sour grape juice. I use it to replace lemon juice as the seasons move. The availability of imported lemons has meant that the use of verjuice has gotten lost, but it is a valuable way to be a little more sustainable. Crushed unripe green grapes taste incredibly similar to lemon juice and can be used wherever you want that 'high note' of gentle acidity that lemon juice provides. I make it fresh as required, but it can have citric acid added to increase its shelf life. You can even freeze it.

If you have a grape vine and are thinning the grape bundles, or know of a vineyard that is doing that, then this is a perfect use. Thinning the grape bundles is usually done to increase the quality of the remaining ones. I have birds doing this for me, but that's another story. The best time to pick the grapes is the moment they start to colour, which is when they are very close to full size. If you just want a little juice over the top of your salad, pop one or two grapes into a garlic crusher. This can also be done with crab apples, if you happen to have a tree.

•

Remove the grapes from their stems and crush them. This can be done in a bowl with a potato masher, or through a food mill. I tend to use the former so that I don't crush the pips.

You end up with slurry of skins, pips and juice. It oxidises quite quickly to a muddy colour, so try and work fast to retain the colour. Either press through a sieve, or bundle everything into a muslin cloth and squeeze the juice into a bowl. You could also run it through paper towel to take any of the finer sediment out, but that is only necessary for appearances.

It will last like this for a couple of days in the fridge. If you would like it to last longer, stir in the citric acid. This will make it last up to 6 months, though the colour will become brown.

Vegetable Stock

1 onion, or the equivalent in
    peelings
30g parsley stalks or fresh parsley
1 carrot, or the equivalent in
    peelings
1 celery stalk and leaves
Parmesan rind (any size chunk
    that is leftover)

While a lot of kitchen scraps are perfect for the compost, you can use some of them in a simple vegetable stock. It's a great way to save a dollar or two, and to have as one of your kitchen basics.

It has become a kitchen habit of mine to pop clean vegetable scraps into a lidded container in the fridge for a few days until there is enough to work with. I always do a little wander around the garden and gather a few herbs to add. I use this same container of scraps for chicken stock with my leftover roast chicken frame. The longer you cook this and reduce it, the stronger the flavour. Having a smaller amount means it will take up less space in your freezer, and you can add water to it again when you go to use it.

•

Roughly chop everything and place into a large saucepan. Add 2 litres water and bring to the boil, then reduce the heat and simmer for an hour or so.

Strain and use immediately, or freeze in portions. You can freeze it in ice cube trays, then remove and store in a bag or container in the freezer so you can reuse your ice cube tray.

These cubes are perfect for adding to a huge range of dishes, even just for cooking rice.

•

NOTE: If you have peelings or pieces left from parsnip, leek or other herbs, feel free to add them to the mix.

Simple Nut Butter

MAKES A 500G JAR

500g shelled macadamias (or
    another nut of your choice)
½ tsp sea salt (or to taste)

My macadamia trees double as garage-hiding boundary trees, slowly replacing a fast growing tree used to screen the neighbours' place. So they work double duty – screening and food. I thought they would be tricky or needy, but they turned out to be easier than I thought.

I hadn't heard, known or read much about nut trees in everyday gardens, so I cautiously started with macadamias, mainly because I like to bake with them. The little trees that came home in the footwell of my car doubled in size every year, and were bigger than the car in less than three years. The only advice on the label was to avoid high winds, but mine face the full force of the Manukau Harbour in defiance of the instructions, and survived! Now they intoxicate a huge number of bees with their honey-scented flowers.

Macadamia trees are susceptible to guava moth, which is a nuisance as I don't spray with insecticides. The affected nuts fall early, so I have become religious about removing them. They can't be composted, but make great fire kindling.

•

Preheat the oven to 150°C fan-forced.

Spread nuts in a single layer onto a large baking tray with a rim. Place into the oven and roast for about 10 minutes (but keep an eye on them), until lightly golden. Set aside to cool.

Transfer to a blender (or food processor) and blend on a medium speed for a few moments to break up the nuts. Turn up to high speed, and blend for about 10 minutes, stopping to scrape down the sides frequently, until completely smooth. You need to make sure the nuts have released their oil before you stop. Add salt to taste.

If you would like a crunchy texture, keep some of the original toasted nuts aside and add them at the very end, with a quick blitz just to mix them through evenly. Store in a sterilised jar (see page 249).

•

NOTE: If making a smaller batch, you can roast the nuts in a dry frying pan over low heat, rather than turning on the oven.

Pasta

SERVES 6

4 cups (600g) 00 flour
5 eggs
½ tbsp olive oil

The thing about pasta, in my family at least, is that it is the number one way to eat less meat. They truly don't seem to notice when I've combined fresh homemade pasta with garden goodies, such as peas and parmesan or tomato and anchovy, or even something as simple as basil pesto tossed through with a little cracked pepper on top.

•

Place the flour into a mound on the bench and make a well in the centre. Add the eggs and the olive oil. Using a fork (or by hand) slowly start to mix the eggs and the oil, incorporating the flour on the inside of the mound as you go.

The dough will slowly start to come together. Once the flour has all been incorporated, start kneading the dough with the heel of your hand. If it is sticky, add a little flour to the bench and continue to knead for a good 10 minutes. The dough should be soft, elastic and just a little sticky.

Cover with a damp cloth and let it rest for 30 minutes.

Cut the dough into 8 pieces. Shape 1 piece into a rough rectangular shape and dust generously with flour. Starting on the widest setting of the rollers on the pasta machine, feed the dough through. Fold into thirds and feed it through again the other way (starting at the shortest side). Do this a couple of times, dusting with flour as necessary.

Change to the next setting on the pasta machine, and roll the dough through. Change to the next setting and roll again, without folding. Keep rolling, reducing the setting each time and finishing at your desired thickness (it will depend on how you are going to use the pasta). Repeat with the remaining dough and cut into desired shapes.

NOTE: For pasta sauce inspirations, see Asparagus & Lemon Ricotta Ravioli (page 18), Pestos (pages 54–5), pasta and Marinara Sauces (page 102–3), and Butternut Cappellacci with Browned Butter & Sage Sauce (page 124).

Gnocchi

1kg floury potatoes, scrubbed
(try to choose similar sizes)
1½ cups (375g) plain flour
1 egg
1 tsp salt
½ cup (125ml) oil (light oil, such
as rice bran or canola)

Gnocchi makes a wonderful companion to garden vegetables or herbs. Honestly, gnocchi pan fried in brown butter topped with fresh sage is a meal on its own. Another favourite easy topping is spinach with cream and garlic. Gnocchi is a recipe that is soothing to make, and the feeling of accomplishment when you've also grown the potatoes is quite another level.

•

Place the potatoes into a large saucepan and cover with cold water. Bring slowly to the boil, then cook for about 30 minutes, or until tender when pierced with a skewer.

Drain potatoes and cool slightly. While they are still warm (but not too hot to handle), peel off the skins. Press potatoes through a potato ricer, vegetable mill or through a wire sieve onto the board or bench you plan on continuing working on.

Mound the potatoes and make a well in the centre. Sprinkle with the flour. Break the egg into the well, and add the salt. Using a fork (or by hand), slowly stir the egg while incorporating the potato and flour from the inside of the mound. Once everything is mixed, gather the dough into a ball and gently knead for 5 minutes, until smooth.

Divide the dough into 6 portions. Working one at a time, roll each portion into a rope about 2cm thick, then cut into pieces about the size of the top half of your thumb. At this point you can roll the pieces over a fork for the serrated shape, or leave them as they are.

Cook the gnocchi (in batches, so you don't overcrowd the pan) in a large saucepan of boiling water. They are ready when they float to the surface. If using straight away, use a slotted spoon to transfer to your sauce (which you will have ready and warm in a frying pan).

If you want to cook the gnocchi ahead of time, transfer to a bowl of iced water. Drain well, then toss in a light oil and keep, covered, in the fridge for up to 2 days. To serve, add to your heated sauce and toss to reheat.

Carte di Musica

MAKES 10–12

2 cups (300g) 00 flour
¾ cup (120g) fine semolina
1 tsp salt
1 cup (250ml) water
Extra virgin olive oil, to brush
Sea salt, to taste

Carte di musica are a flat bread or cracker that are 'as thin as a sheet of music', hence the name. These are very simple and usually just flavoured with salt, but you could get creative and add parmesan, seeds or herbs from the garden, pressing them lightly onto the raw rolled dough before baking. Keep them in your pantry to serve with any antipasti or evening drinks (in Italy, they are often served in bars with warmed olives). We've always served them with dips and spreads.

•

Preheat the oven to 220–250°C fan-forced (or as hot as your oven will go).

Combine the dry ingredients in a large mixing bowl. Gradually add the water, using a fork to slowly mix together until you have a soft (but not sticky) dough. Rest the dough for 10 minutes.

Divide dough into 10–12 portions. For each portion, roll dough through the widest pasta setting on your pasta machine, fold in half and feed it through again on a narrower setting.The first run might appear a bit raggedy, but it will improve with each fold and roll through the pasta machine.

Keep rolling, reducing the setting each time, until you have a fine 'paper thin' sheet (If the dough tears or breaks just fold and re-roll it). Repeat with remaining dough. Place onto large baking trays. Brush with a little olive oil and sprinkle with sea salt. Bake for 8–10 minutes, until crisp and lightly golden. Transfer to a wire rack to cool.

Store in an airtight container. They will keep for several weeks, but if they seem a bit stale pop them in a 160°C oven for 5 minutes.

Garden-Inspired

Jams

Magnolia Petal

MAKES A 250ML JAR

150g water
150g sugar
50g magnolia petals, chopped
    just before adding
20g lemon juice

When I found that magnolia petals are not only edible, but inexplicably delicious, I made a syrup then took it one step further to this glorious jam. It is so simple and yet the finished product tastes like there were more ingredients than there actually are. There are so many edible flowers that I was (and still am) unaware of. I have made many attempts with different plants to tease out their flowers' scent as a flavour, but a lot of flowers do not indulge this. This is one of the exceptions – the jam tastes like sweet floral ginger. If you don't have a magnolia tree, I highly recommend foraging for a bundle of petals. Try to choose ones that don't have too many brown edges – this happens quickly, so you will need to use them the same day.

•

Combine the water and sugar in a heavy-based saucepan. Stir over low heat to dissolve the sugar then increase the heat to medium and bring to the boil. Add the chopped petals and lemon juice. Cook for about 20 minutes, or until it reaches setting point.

Transfer to sterilised jars (see below), seal tightly and leave to cool. Keep in a cool, dark place for up to 3 months. Once opened, store in the fridge.

•

NOTE: Make sure you chop the petals just before adding to the syrup or the edges will become brown.

TIP: To test if setting point has been reached, remove pan from heat and spoon a little onto a chilled saucer and let cool for a minute. If the jam wrinkles when pushed with your fingertip, it is ready.

STERILISING JARS

To sterilise jars or bottles for preserving, give them a good wash then put them on a tray in the oven at 120°C for 10 minutes.

Strawberry & Black Pepper

MAKES 3 × 500ML JARS

1kg strawberries (fresh or frozen)
Juice of 2 lemons
1kg jam setting sugar
1 tsp butter
3 tsp cracked black pepper

Place the strawberries into a large heavy-based saucepan with the lemon juice over low heat. Bring to a simmer and cook for 15 minutes, stirring occasionally, until the fruit has fully softened.

Add the sugar and cook, stirring occasionally, until the sugar has dissolved. Add the butter, increase the heat to medium-high and bring to a rapid boil. Cook for 15 minutes or until it reaches setting point. Stir in the pepper.

Leave to cool for about 15 minutes, then skim any froth from the top. Place into sterilised jars (see page 249), seal tightly and leave to cool.

Keep in a cool dark place for up to 6 months. Once opened, store in the fridge.

Rhubarb & Ginger

MAKES A 500ML JAR

400g rhubarb, diced
400g sugar
20g piece fresh ginger, finely grated
2 pieces crystalised ginger, finely diced
½ lemon

Mix all the ingredients together in a large heavy-based saucepan. Leave to stand for an hour or so for the flavours to combine.

Place over low heat and stir to dissolve the sugar. Increase the heat to medium and bring to the boil. Cook for about 20 minutes or until it reaches setting point. Add a squeeze of lemon towards the end of cooking time.

Place into sterilised jars (see page 249), seal tightly and leave to cool. Keep in a cool dark place for up to 6 months. Once opened, store in the fridge.

Mandarin & Amaretto Marmalata

MAKES 6 × 500ML JARS

1.5kg mandarins
3 litres cold water
3kg sugar
Juice of 1 lemon
150ml amaretto (see page 216)

I love mandarins. I have two mandarin trees, one fruits early and has a tight skin, the other fruits a little later with an easy-peel skin. I use the tight-skinned mandarins for this recipe as it is a little easier to handle them.

.

Place the fruit in a saucepan with the water. Bring to a simmer and cook gently for about 45 minutes, or until the skins are easily pierced. Remove from the heat and leave to cool.

Preheat the oven to 150°C. Cut each fruit in half and remove any pips. Finely slice, on a board over bowl if possible to catch the juice. Place the fruit (and juice) back into the water.

Warm the sugar on a rimmed tray in the oven for 10 minutes, then add it to the saucepan, along with the lemon juice. Heat gently over medium-low heat, stirring slowly to dissolve the sugar.

Once dissolved, bring to the boil and cook vigorously for 10 minutes, until it reaches setting point.

Remove from the heat and stir in the amaretto. Place into sterilised jars (see page 249), seal tightly and leave to cool.

Keep in a cool dark place for up to 6 months. Once opened, store in the fridge.

Mandarin 'Honey'

MAKES A 250ML JAR

2 mandarins, zest finely grated, juiced
2 egg yolks
120g sugar
120g butter

This is a great way to extend a small harvest, or to make delicious treats to gift. This is a more intensely flavoured version than most, but worth the effort for the finished result. Mandarin happens to be my favourite – lemon is a good substitute. In fact, you could use any of your favourite citrus.

.

Combine the ingredients in a saucepan or double boiler and stir constantly over low heat until it thickens. Do not allow it to boil.

Transfer to a sterilised jar (see page 249) and keep in the fridge for up to 2 weeks.

Smoothies

Smoothies are a delicious way to use small harvests of fresh produce from your garden, perhaps extending a handful of strawberries to serve more than just one person. I have little silicon ice block moulds that I use for any leftover smoothie mixture to have on hand for a summer afternoon treat. I often remove the ice block, enclose it in baking paper and write the flavour on outside. This frees up the moulds to use again. If you are using leftovers in this way, you end up with a great range of ice blocks to choose from over summer. A lot of these recipes could be juices, but smoothies give you a little more fibre in your diet.

SERVES 2

Blend all ingredients until smooth, then serve split between two glasses.

Creamy Mandarin

2 mandarins, peeled (or an orange)
1 frozen chopped banana
½ tsp cocoa powder
Small handful of cashews
1–2 cups (250–500ml) milk (any type)

Green Avocado

½ avocado
1½ cups spinach leaves, chopped
1 frozen chopped banana
2 cups (500ml) coconut milk
A few fresh mint leaves

Green Ginger

1 frozen chopped banana
½ cucumber, roughly chopped
Small piece fresh ginger, to taste
2 cups spinach leaves, chopped
2 cups (500ml) coconut water

Tomato

2 tomatoes, chopped
1 stick celery. chopped
1 tsp honey
2 tsp lime juice
1 cup (250ml) water or coconut water
Pinch cayenne pepper or chopped jalapeno
    (if you want some spice)

Feijoa

4 feijoas, flesh scooped out
1 frozen chopped banana
½ tsp ground cinnamon
1 apple, cored and diced
1 tbsp maple syrup
2 cups (500ml) coconut water or water

OTHER SMOOTHIE COMBINATIONS

Strawberries, honey & lemon balm

Apple, mint, coconut water & lime juice

Feijoa, kiwifruit & oat milk

Passionfruit, mint & yoghurt

Mandarin & maple syrup

Tomato, chilli & honey

Avocado, mint & coconut cream

Fig, honey & yoghurt

Marinades

These marinades are equally at home being used on chicken, beef, lamb or pork, as they are on tofu, potatoes, cauliflower or many root vegetables and pulses. I often marinate meat before freezing. I cut it into ready-to-cook sizes, toss in the marinade and freeze in an airtight bag. Then it is just a matter of defrosting and cooking for a quick 'serve with rice' kind of dinner. My absolute favourite in this collection is a marinade I've dubbed Singapore pork (see page 259), because that's what I usually use it on. It works just as well with chicken or even cauliflower.

All you need to do for the basic marinades is to combine the ingredients, though the Chimichurri, Tandoori and Singapore marinades take a tiny bit more preparation. I've used olive oil, but feel free to use avocado oil or any preferred oil.

MAKES ENOUGH FOR 4 PORTIONS

Italian

½ cup (125ml) olive oil
¼ cup (60ml) balsamic vinegar
3 garlic cloves, crushed
4 basil leaves, finely chopped
2 stems oregano, leaves finely chopped
½ chilli, finely chopped

Citrus & Soy

¼ cup (60ml) olive oil
¼ cup (60ml) orange juice
¼ cup (60ml) light soy sauce
Finely grated ginger, to taste
Finely chopped coriander, to taste

Spicy Lime

¼ cup (60ml) lime juice
¼ cup (60ml) olive oil
1 tsp honey
1 garlic clove, crushed
1 chilli, finely chopped
1 tsp ground cumin
½ tsp smoked paprika

Orange & Sesame

¼ cup (60ml) olive oil
1 tbsp sesame oil
¼ cup (60ml) orange juice
1 tsp finely grated orange zest
1 garlic clove, crushed
1 tsp finely grated ginger

Tomato & Basil

½ cup (125ml) tomato puree
1 fresh tomato, blended until smooth
½ cup (125ml) olive oil
Handful of basil leaves, finely chopped
1 garlic clove, crushed
1 tsp honey
¼ tsp paprika

Chilli & Coconut

¼ cup (60ml) coconut milk
¼ cup (60ml) light soy sauce
1 jalapeno, seeded and finely chopped
1 tbsp honey
1 tsp finely grated lime zest
1 tsp lime juice

Pesto

Handful of basil, finely chopped
¼ cup (60ml) olive oil
1 tsp very finely grated Parmesan
1 tsp almond meal
1 garlic clove, crushed

Jalapeno & Honey

½ cup (125ml) olive oil
1 tbsp rice vinegar
1 tbsp brown sugar
2 tsp honey
3 garlic cloves, crushed
1 jalapeno, seeded and finely chopped

Rosemary & Balsamic

½ cup (125ml) balsamic vinegar
½ cup (125ml) olive oil
2 garlic cloves, crushed
2 tbsp honey
2 tbsp finely chopped parsley
1 tsp finely chopped rosemary

Apple & Soy

1 apple, cored and grated
3 garlic cloves, crushed
1 tsp sesame oil
¼ cup (60ml) light soy sauce
1 tbsp honey
1 spring onion, finely chopped

Lemon & Garlic

½ cup (125ml) olive oil
1 lemon, zest finely grated, juiced
5 garlic cloves, crushed
¼ tsp sea salt
2 tsp finely chopped basil
1 tsp finely chopped oregano

Apple & Fennel

¼ cup (60ml) olive oil
¼ cup (60ml) apple cider vinegar
2 sprigs thyme, leaves finely chopped
1 tsp fennel seeds, crushed
½ tsp sea salt
½ apple, grated

Miso & Chilli

3 tsp miso paste
1 tsp finely grated ginger
1 chilli, finely chopped
1 tsp honey
1 tsp sesame oil
¼ cup (60ml) olive oil

Mandarin 5 Spice

½ cup (125ml) mandarin juice
1 tsp finely grated mandarin zest
1 tsp sesame oil
1 tsp 5 spice powder
1 small chilli, finely chopped
¼ cup (60ml) sake
2 garlic cloves, crushed

Chimichurri

1 cup flat-leaf parsley leaves and
    soft stems, finely chopped
¼ cup coriander leaves and soft
    stems, finely chopped
¼ cup oregano leaves, finely
    chopped
4 garlic cloves, finely chopped
½ red onion, finely chopped
½ cup (125ml) olive oil
⅓ cup (80ml) fresh lemon juice
¼ cup (60ml) red wine vinegar
Pinch of dried chilli flakes

To get the best consistency, use a mortar and pestle to mix the herbs, garlic and onion to a paste. This really blends the flavours well. If you don't have a mortar and pestle you can skip this step.

Transfer to a bowl and whisk in the oil, juice and vinegar. Season with chilli flakes and salt and pepper to taste. Keep in the fridge for up to 3 days.

NOTE: This is just as delicious served on scrambled eggs or crostini as on a steak.

Tandoori

10 cloves
10 cardamom pods
2 tsp coriander seeds
2 tsp cumin seeds
2 onions, roughly chopped
50g ginger, roughly chopped
4 garlic cloves
¼ cup (70g) plain yoghurt
1 ½ tsp ground turmeric
2 tsp ground black pepper
2 tsp chilli powder

Roast the cloves, cardamom, coriander and cumin seeds in a dry frying pan over medium heat for about a minute, or until aromatic. Cool, then coarsely grind.

Place the onions, ginger and garlic in a food processor and process until smooth. Add the remaining ingredients (including ground spices) and pulse briefly a couple of times to combine.

Singapore Pork

1 tbsp coriander seeds
5 small shallots, roughly chopped
1 stalk lemongrass (pale part),
    roughly chopped
½ cup (125ml) olive oil
1 tbsp brown sugar
1 tsp salt
½ tsp ground turmeric

Lightly toast the coriander seeds in a dry frying pan over medium heat for about a minute, or until aromatic. Cool, then grind to a powder.

Place the shallots and lemongrass in a blender and blend until a paste is formed. Add the oil and blend until combined. Transfer to a bowl and combine with the other ingredients.

Syrups

These syrups are lovely to have on hand for to add flavour to sodas, glazes, iced teas, icing for cakes or just sweet drizzles over fruit or fruit salads.

Base Syrup

MAKES ABOUT 1 LITRE

350g sugar
600ml water

Combine the sugar and water in a large saucepan and stir over medium heat until sugar has dissolved. Bring to the boil.

Remove from the heat and add the flavouring ingredients for your syrup (see list below – the quantity depends on how strong you want the flavour). Gently stir the ingredients for a moment, then return to the stove over very low heat and simmer for 5–10 minutes.

Set aside to cool and for the mixture to steep. Once cooled, strain and transfer to a sterilised bottle (see page 249). Keep in the fridge for up to 3 months.

OTHER SYRUP COMBINATIONS

These are some flavour suggestions, but you can make the most of what is happening in your garden. I often combine a fruit with a herb, but there are no hard and fast rules to this.

Lime zest & vanilla

Ginger & pear

Sage & lemon

Fennel & clove

Lemon verbena, ginger & honey

Mandarin & 5 spice

Mint & strawberry

Peach & vanilla

Rose petal & raspberry

Lavender & thyme

Rosemary & lemon or lime

Rhubarb & cinnamon

Mint & apple

Fig Leaf

MAKES 500ML

1 cup (220g) sugar
1 cup (250ml) water
5 small to medium fig leaves
 (not fully mature older ones)
1 tsp finely grated lemon zest
 (or ½ tsp vanilla extract if
 you prefer)

Combine the sugar and water in a saucepan and stir over low heat to dissolve the sugar. Add the fig leaves and lemon zest. Bring to a simmer and cook gently for 10 minutes.

Pour into a bowl, cover and leave overnight. Strain into a sterilised bottle (see page 249).

Keep in the fridge for up to 3 months.

Magnolia Petal

MAKES 500ML

1 cup (220g) sugar
1 cup (250ml) water
50g petals (pink are best), chopped
 just before adding

Combine the sugar and water in a saucepan and stir over low heat to dissolve the sugar. Add the petals. Bring to a simmer and cook gently for 20 minutes, stirring occasionally.

Set aside to cool and steep. Strain the petals out (they are delicious to eat). Transfer to a sterilised bottle (see page 249).

Keep in the fridge for several weeks.

♦

NOTE: Make sure you don't chop the petals until just before adding to the syrup or the edges will become brown.

Lemon, Lime & Bitters

2 limes (see note)
2 lemons
1 cup (250ml) fresh lime juice
1 cup (250ml) fresh lemon juice
500g white sugar
2 cups (500ml) water
5 tsp Angostura bitters, or to taste
20g citric acid

As my citrus trees took off I had to find new ways of using the fruit, as there is only so much lemon curd and preserved lemon that I can use. This makes a refreshing drink in soda water, but can also be used as a base other recipes or salad dressings.

•

Use a small sharp knife or vegetable peeler to cut the zest of the lemons and limes, with as little of the white pith as possible.

Combine the zest and 1 cup of the sugar in a blender. Blitz until the sugar has a breadcrumb-like texture.

Transfer to a saucepan and add the remaining ingredients (except bitters). Stir over low heat, without boiling, to dissolve the sugar.

Remove from the heat and add the bitters a little at a time, tasting as you go to find your preferred flavour. Stir in the citric acid.

Strain into glass bottles and store in the fridge for up to 6 months.

To serve, use 15–30ml per portion, topped up with soda or water.

•

NOTE: Juice the lemons and limes after removing the zest, then add more to make up to 1 cup of each.

Shrubs

A shrub is a drinking vinegar, and is often used as a base for a cocktail. It makes a refreshing replacement for the much sweeter additions you would normally use. It's also a great way to experiment with goodies from your garden, as you can use all sorts of things for flavouring. Because they have a vinegar base, the chilled shelf life of these is quite long – easily a month. To serve, mix with soda or prosecco, or just serve over crushed ice.

Rhubarb & Mint

MAKES ABOUT 500ML

1 cup finely chopped ripe rhubarb (well packed)
Whole mint leaves, to taste
1 cup (220g) sugar
1 cup (250ml) red wine vinegar

Toss the rhubarb, mint and sugar together in a bowl. Cover and refrigerate for 3 days, stirring a couple of times a day.

Strain the mixture through a sieve over a bowl. This may take some time so leave it to sit for a while.

Discard the solids and measure the liquid. Add the same quantity of vinegar to the liquid (it may be less than the 1 cup listed).

Pour into a clean jar or bottle and keep in the fridge for up to 2 weeks.

Magnolia Petal & Blueberry

MAKES ABOUT 500ML

10 magnolia petals (preferably pink)
½ cup (75g) blueberries (fresh or frozen)
½ cup (110g) sugar
2 cups (500ml) coconut vinegar

Place all the ingredients into a jar. Seal tightly with the lid and shake well. Refrigerate for 1 week.

Strain then transfer to a clean jar or bottle and store in the fridge for up to 2 weeks.

This is stunning in a champagne cocktail and makes a whimsical brunch drink.

Apple, Cinnamon & Brown Sugar

1½ cups (110g) grated apple
(see note)
¾ cup (165g) brown sugar
½ tsp ground cinnamon
Small slice of fresh ginger (skin on)
1 cup (250ml) apple cider vinegar

Place all the ingredients into a jar. Seal tightly with the lid and shake well. Refrigerate for at least 3 days.

Remove from the fridge and strain through muslin, squeezing out all the liquid.

Transfer to a clean jar or bottle and store in the fridge for up to 2 weeks.

•

NOTE: This is lovely using either sweet apples or more tart cooking apples. It really depends on the flavour you prefer.

Strawberry, Honey & Lemon Balm

2 cups sliced strawberries
1 cup (220g) brown sugar
½ cup (125ml) raw honey
8 leaves lemon balm, slightly
bruised
2 cups (500ml) apple cider vinegar

Place the strawberries, sugar, honey and lemon balm into a large jar. Stand at room temperature for a few hours, then add vinegar.

Refrigerate for a few days or up to a week, then strain into a clean jar and keep refrigerated for up to 2 weeks.

Mandarin, Mint & Balsamic

2 mandarins, peeled and sliced
Whole mint leaves, to taste
½ cup (110g) brown sugar
1 cup (250ml balsamic vinegar

Place the mandarins, mint and sugar into a jar. Set aside for an hour or so, until the sugar dissolves into the juice from the mandarins.

Add the vinegar, seal tightly with the lid and shake well.

Refrigerate for a few days and then strain. Transfer to a clean jar or bottle and store in the fridge for up to 2 weeks.

This is stunning served on ice with rum, or even just ice and soda water.

Index

HarperCollins*Publishers*

Australia • Brazil • Canada • France • Germany • Holland • India
Italy • Japan • Mexico • New Zealand • Poland • Spain • Sweden
Switzerland • United Kingdom • United States of America

First published in 2023
by HarperCollins*Publishers* (New Zealand) Limited
Unit D1, 63 Apollo Drive, Rosedale, Auckland 0632, New Zealand

harpercollins.co.nz

A catalogue record for this book is available
from the National Library of New Zealand

ISBN 978 1 7755 4198 1 (hardback)

Project editor: Shannon Kelly
Publisher: Holly Hunter
Recipe editor: Tracy Rutherford
Cover and internal design by Andy Warren
Front cover image 'Tomato with Whipped Feta' (recipe page 108)
Prop styling by Lottie Hedley
Index by Shannon Kelly
Colour reproduction by Splitting Image Colour Studio, Wantirna,
  Victoria
Printed and bound in China by 1010 on 140gsm woodfree

8 7 6 5 4 3 2 1   23 24 25 26